The Book
Of
Wisdom

(Information Known By A Selected Few)

By
A.J.C.,III

Order this book online at www.trafford.com
or email orders@trafford.com

Most Trafford titles are also available at major online book retailers.

Note for Librarians: A cataloguing record for this book is available from Library
and Archives Canada at www.collectionscanada.ca/amicus/index-e.html

Printed in Victoria, BC, Canada.

ISBN: 978-1-4269-1801-8

*Our mission is to efficiently provide the world's finest, most comprehensive book publishing
service, enabling every author to experience success. To find out how to publish your book, your
way, and have it available worldwide, visit us online at www.trafford.com*

Trafford rev. 09/04/09

 www.trafford.com

North America & international
toll-free: 1 888 232 4444 (USA & Canada)
phone: 250 383 6864 ♦ fax: 812 355 4082

And Jesus

answered and said unto

them, Take heed that no man

deceive you.

St. Matthew

Chapter 24:4

And Jesus came and spake unto them saying,

All power is given unto Me

In Heaven and in earth.

St. Matthew

Chapter 28: 18

As Above, So Below.

But thou, O Daniel, shut up the words,

And seal the book, even to the time

of the end: many shall run

to and fro, and knowledge

shall be increased.

Daniel

Chapter 12: 4

23 MAR 08, BEGINS the writing of this book into its finalized form, but the concepts and ideas have been in my mind for some years. Quite a few well-respected people have presented a lot of research to me. I found some of the research over the years as I studied the Holy Bible and other documents that are well known and some that are obscure or even kept away from the masses. But I feel that due to the fact that I, while in my teenage years, had the unique opportunity to "ride the goat", which I feel has given me the opportunity to have been led into the viewing of hidden knowledge, secret writings and information that many could not or would refuse to understand.

The information that I am about to present to you is actual facts and can be traced to their sources. I could only wish to be so creative as to be able to "make up" something like this. I have even added a chapter where I attempt to show the wisdom that I have learned throughout my life and put them into my own sayings. I call my sayings "DraVerbs", (pronounced with the 'A' sound)

I hope that you can find this information useful to your way of thinking. That it helps you to See a little bit better. This is for your benefit if you choose to use it, and it is a choice, not a demand for you to understand these things that you will see here. If you don't believe what you read, just remind yourself to ask yourself, 'what if it is real?'

Respectfully yours,
A. J. C., III

These writings are considered to be
Advanced Level Teachings,

  But is not to be considered

  The replacement for any of

The information

That we have

Previously

Learned.

Table of Contents

Chapter 1

WE ALL KNOW THE story about the circumstances of the birth of Jesus. We have heard it thousands of times from different sources, such as, Sunday school, church services, TV movies, bedtime stories as kids and so on. But have you ever felt that while hearing them that sometimes there would seem to be missing parts or left out evidence that would make it more believable, or seem to be more fact related. You know, some different points of views by people that would tell their sides of it, were we as inquisitive as we are would be even more equipped to add up the two and two ourselves without being dictated to and told what to believe.

For many years, I have taken it upon my self to learn the things that was not being taught by the information system that we have grown to know. But it's not all their fault; they were only following orders, which were established way before them, as to the point of when they got into the system to learn to be teachers. They were taught well and almost all of them still only teach what they were taught. Advantage…The System.

As a young man, I grew up in a household where my mother and stepfather had ties to and were involved in what many would call a secret society organization. These associations in turn led to my siblings and I "Riding the Goat", which was a form of initiation into that world. I came to realize many years later; that it led to esoteric learning and the revelation of information that is not for everybody to know. I will not reveal all or even most of the information that I have aquired over the years, but I will reveal some interesting documentations that were presented to me and found by me.

These were entered according to Act of Congress in the year 1887 and 1896 by Rev W. D. Mahan in the office of the Librarian of Congress, at Washington, D. C., in a book published by the PHILADELPHIA: ANTIQUARIAN BOOK COMPANY. 1905. It's known as The ARCHKO VOLUM; or, THE ARCHEOLOGICAL WRITINGS OF THE SANHEDRIM AND TALMUDS OF THE JEWS. (INTRA SECUS) THESE ARE THE OFFICIAL DOCUMENTS MADE IN THESE COURTS IN THE DAYS OF JESUS CHRIST. TRANSLATED BY Drs. McINTOSH AND TWYMAN, of the ANTIQUARIAN LODGE, GENOA, ITALY. FROM MANUSCRIPTS IN

1

CONSTANINOPLE AND THE RECORDS OF THE SENATORIAL DOCKET TAKEN FROM THE VATICAN AT ROME.

Lets begin with what happened, pertaining to the date of, as the calendar we know calls that month
April 19th, 6 B.C.
The actual birth date of the Anointed One.
Eight months before the Magi arrived from what is now known as Iraq.

Jonathan's Interview

Jonathan's Interview with the Bethlehem
Shepherds-Letter of MELKER, PRIEST OF
THE SYNAGOGUE AT BETHLEHEM.

Sanhedrim, 88 B. By R. Jose Order No. 2

Jonathan, son of Heziel, questions the shepherds and others at Bethlehem in regard to the strange circumstances reported to have occurred there, and reports to this court:

"Jonathan to the Masters of Israel, Servants of the True God ": In obedience to your order, I met with two men, who said they were shepherds, and were watching their flocks near Bethlehem. They told me that while attending to their sheep, the night being cold and chilly, some of them had made fires to warm themselves, and some of them had laid down and were asleep; that they were awaken by those who were keeping watch with the question, "What does this all mean? Behold, how light it is! That where they were aroused it was light as day. But they knew it was not daylight, for it was only the third watch. All at once the air seemed to be filled with human voices, saying, 'Glory! Glory! Glory to the most high God!' and, 'Happy art thou, Bethlehem, for God hath fulfilled His promise to the fathers; for in thy chambers is born the King that shall rule in righteousness.' Their shoutings would rise up in the heavens, and then would sink down in mellow strains, and roll along at the foot of the mountains, and die away in the most soft and musical manner they had ever heard; then it would begin again high up in the heavens, in the very vaults of the sky, and descend in sweet and melodious strains, so that they could not refrain from shouting and weeping at the same time. The light would seem to burst forth high up in the heavens, and then decend in softer rays and light up the hills and valleys, making everything more visible than the light of the sun, though it was not so brilliant, but clearer, like the brightness of the moon. I asked them how they felt-if they were afraid; they said at first they were; but after awhile it seemed to calm their spirits, and so filled their hearts with love and tranquillity that they felt more like giving thanks than anything else. They said that it was around the whole city, and some of the people were almost scared to death. Some said that the world was on fire; some said the gods were coming down to destroy them; others said a star had fallen; until Melker the priest came out shouting and clapping his hands, seeming to be frantic with joy. The people all came crowding around him, and he told them that it was the sign that God was coming to fulfil His promise made to their father Abraham. He told us that fourteen hundred years before God had appeared to Abraham, and told him to put all Israel under bonds--sacred bonds of obedience; and if they would be faithful, He would give them a Saviour to redeem them from sin, and that he would give them eternal life, and that they should hunger no more; that the time of their suffering should cease forever; and that the sign of His coming would be that light that would shine from on high, and the angels would announce His coming, and their voices should be heard in the city, and the people should rejoice: and a virgin that was pure should travail in pain and bring fourth her first born, and He should rule all flesh by sanctifying it and making it obedient. After Melker had addressed the people in a loud voice, he and all the old Jews went into the synagogue and remained there praising God and giving thanks.

"I went to see Melker, who related to me much the same as the shepherds had reported. He told me that he had lived in India, and that his father had been a priest at Antioch; that he had studied the scrolls of God all his life, and that he knew that the time had come, from signs given, for God to visit and save the Jews from the Roman oppression and from their sins; and as evidence he showed me many quotations on the tripod respecting the matter. "He said that next day three strangers from a great distance called on him, and went in search of this young child; and they found Him and His mother in the mouth of the cave, where there was a shed projecting out for the sheltering of sheep; that His mother was married to a man named Joseph (surname or last name Jacaba), and she related to them the history of her child, saying that an angel had visited her, and told her that she should have a son, and she should call Him Yeshua, (the English translation is Jesus), for He should redeem his people from their sins; and he should call her blessed forever more."

"Whether this is true or not remains to be proved in the future. There have been so many imposters in the world, so many babes born under pretended miracles, and all have proved to be a failure, that this one may be false, this woman only wishing to hide her shame or court the favor of the Jews.

"I am informed that she will be tried by our law, and, if she can give no better evidence of her virtue than she has given to Melker, she will be stoned according to our law, although, as Melker says, there never has been a case before with such apparent divine manifestations as were seen on this occasion. In the past, in various instances, virgins have pretended to be with child by the Holy Ghost, but at the time of their delivery there was no light from the heavens, and no angels talking among the clouds and declaring that this was the King of the Jews. And, as to the truth of these things, the whole of the people of Bethlehem testify to having seen it, and the Roman guard also came out and asked what it meant, and they showed by their actions that they were very much alarmed. These things, Melker says, are all declared in the Scriptures to be the sign of His coming. Melker is a man of great learning and well versed in the prophecies, and he sends you this letter, referring you to those prophecies;"

" 'Melker, Priest of the Synagogue of Bethlehem, to
the Higher Sanhedrim of the Jews at Jerusalem:"

" 'HOLY MASTERS OF ISRAEL: I, your servant, would call your attention to the words of the prophet in regard to the forerunner, and the rise as well as the conductor of a great and mighty nation, wherein should dwell the true principles of righteousness and the conductor of the outward formation of a national domain of God upon earth. As evidence of the fact, the vision and affliction that has befallen Zacharias of late is enough to satisfy all men of the coming of some great event; and this babe of Elizabeth is the beginning of better times.

What has occurred here in the last few days, as Jonathan will inform you, forever settles the question that the day of our redemption is drawing nigh. The sections of these divisions are three: First, the general survey; the original foundation and destiny of man in his single state; the proto-evangel; the full development of mankind; the promises to the fathers of the covenant people; Judah, the leader tribe; section second, the Mosaic law and the Mosaic outlook; the prophecy of Baalam; section third, the anointed one; and the prophets of the past exile: Haggai, Zechariah, and Malachi; Malachi's prophecy of the forerunner of the Lord. Now, noble masters of Israel, if you will refer to the several sections of the divine word, you will not fail to see that all that has been spoken by the prophets in regard to the works of God upon earth has been fulfilled in the last few days in the two events, the birth of the child of Elizabeth and that of Miriam (Mary, niece of Joseph DeMormar who lived in Arimathaea) of Bethlehem.

The unlimited freedom which some men take with these Holy writings of God, as to the above prophecy, subjects us to the severest criticism. It is, however, most satisfactory of the sacred oracles are in no way dependent on the solution of carnal critics, but rest on an inward light shining everywhere out of the bosom of a profound organic unity and a interconnected relation with a consistent and united teleology; overleaping all time, the historical present as well as the past, and all the past brought to light in these two events that have just transpired. Indeed, all past time is blending with the present horizon, and the works of God in ages past are just beginning to develop themselves at this particular time, and the present scenes are bringing us close on to the ways of God upon earth. While we reverence these men of God, we should not misquote their language. Take, for example, the third section of Isaiah, where he prophesies of the captive Israelites, instead of his consolation to the captive. While one of his words refers to the future condition and the reason therefore, the other is sweet in consolation of the Israelites while in this state of captivity and full of the blessed promises in the future.

But let the spirit of prophecy bear us on with the prophet into the future time, far beyond the kingdoms of this world into a glorious future, regardless of the Roman,

Babylonian, or even the Maccabeean rule or rulers; but never forgetting that the prophet is one who is divinely inspired, and is called, commissioned, and qualified to declare the will as well as the knowledge of God. Yes, he is a seer. His prophecy is of the nature of a vision, involving and enveloping all the faculties of the soul, and placing the prophet in the attitude to God of being outside the body and independent of it. Yea, far better without the body than with it; for the further the soul gets from the body the more active it becomes. This fact is demonstrated in our dreams. The vivid powers of the soul are much more active in dreams than at any other time, the perception is clearer, and the sensitive faculties are much more alive when asleep than when awake. We see this verified in the man dying. His eye is usually brighter, his mind is clearer, his soul is freer and less selfish, as he passes on and nears the eternal state.

So is the prophet. He becomes so personal with God that he uses the personalities with seeming presumption; while it is the indwelling power of God's spirit inflating the soul and setting the tongue on fire. So was the moving language of the words to which you have been referred. It seems to me those men of God saw distinctly the gathering light; they saw the travailing of the virgin, they saw the helpless infant in the sheep trough; they heard the mighty chanting of the heavenly host; they saw the ambition of human nature in the Roman soldiery aiming to destroy the child's life; and in that infant they saw human nature in its fallen and helpless condition; and it appears as if they saw the advance of that infant into perfect manhood. As he becomes the theme of the world, his advancing nature will triumph over all; as he does escape the Roman authority this day, so he will finally triumph over all the world, and even death itself shall be destroyed.

We, as Jews, place too much confidence in the outward appearance, while the idea we get of the kingdom of heaven is all of a carnal nature, consisting of forms and ceremonies. The prophecies referred to, and many other passages that I might mention, all go to show that the kingdom of God is to begin within us, in the inner, and rule there, and from the inner nature all outward actions are to flow in conformity with the revealed and written teachings and commands of God. So is the spirit of prophecy. While it uses the natural organs of speech, it at the same time controls all the faculties of life, producing sometimes a real ecstasy, not mechanical or loss of consciousness, though cut off for the time from external relations. He is thus circumscribed to speak, as did Baalam, the words of God with human life. This is to be held by us Jews as of the first and greatest importance, and we are to remember that His prophecy has the same reference to the future that it does to the past, and has respect to the whole empire of man. While it specifies individuals and nations, it often has reference to doctrines and principles; and in this light Israel is the result of prophecy, as a nation with her religious teachings. So is this virgin's babe born to be ruler of all nations of the earth. The Torah itself goes back to prophecy, as well as every prophet stands on the Torah, and on this rests all prophecy pronouncing condemnation on the disobedient and blessing on the faithful. It was on this principle that the covenant of inheritance was made with Abraham, and, in reality, so made David. Thus all the promises, political, ethical, judicial, and ritual, rest on the Torah. In short, the whole administration finds its authority in the prophetic vision, as set forth by the commands of God, to regulate human life – commencing the inner life and working outward, until the outward is like the inward; and thus advancing on from individuals to nations.

The Messianic prophecy has no other justification than this. On this rests the church, and on this rests the theocracy. On this rests the glory of the future kingdom of God upon earth.

The whole chain of prophecy is fulfilled in this babe; but the development is only commencing. He will abolish the old cultus forever, but with man it will develop commensurate with time itself. There are many types in the shadow, in the plant, in the animal. Every time the Romans celebrated a triumph on the Tiber it shadowed forth the coming Caesar; so every suffering of David, or lamentation of Job, or glory of Solomon – yea, every wail of human sorrow, every throe of human grief, every dying sigh, every falling bitter tear – was a type, a prophecy of the coming King of the Jews and the Savior of the world. Israel stands as a common factor at every great epoch of history. The shading of the colors of the prophetic painting does not obliterate the prediction of the literal Israel's more glorious future in the Kingdom of God. Her historic calling to mediate salvation to the nations is not ended with this new-comer on the stage of earthly life. The prophecy is eschatological, refining the inner life as well as shaping the outer life in conformity to good laws. Looking also to the end of time and its great importance to us, it has something to teach, and we have something to learn. Along the ages past all the great, good, and happy have first learned their duties, and then performed them; and thus for thousands of years Israel has stood, hope never dying in the Hebrew heart, and has been the only appointed source of preserved knowledge of the true God. And this day she stands as the great factor and centre around which all nations of the earth must come for instruction to guide them, that they may become better and happier.

These sacred scrolls which we Jews received from God by the hand of Moses are the only hope of the world. If they were lost to mankind, it be worst than putting out the sun, moon, and all the stars of night, for this would be a loss of sacred light to the souls of men. When we consider the surroundings, there never has been a time more propitious than the present for the establishing of the true religion, and it seems, by reviewing our history for hundreds of years past, that this is the time for the ushering in of the true kingdom of God. The nations of the earth that have been given to idolatry are growing tired of placing confidence in and depending on gods that do not help them in the hour of danger, and they are now wanting a God that can and will answer their calls.

King Herod sent for me the other day, and after I related to him of the God of the Jews and His works, of the many and mighty deeds He had performed for our fathers and for us as a nation, he seemed to think, if there was such a God as we professed, it was far better than to depend on such gods as the Romans had made, of timber, stone, and iron; and ever the gods of gold were powerless. He said that if he could know that this babe that was declared by the angels, was such a God as He that saved the Israelites in the Red Sea, and saved Daniel, and those from the fearful heat of fire, he would have pursued quite a different course toward him. He was under the impression that he had come to drive the Romans from their possessions, and to reign as a monarch instead of Caesar. And I find this to be the general feeling throughout the world, so far as I can hear; that the people want and are ready to receive a God that can demonstrate in his life that He is such a God that the race of men can depend on in time of trouble; and if He can show such power to His friends He will be feared by His enemies, and thus become universally obeyed by all nations of the earth. And this, I fear, is going to be a trouble with our nation; our people are going to look to Him as a temporal deliverer, and will aim to circumscribe him to the Jews alone; and His actions begin to flow out to all the inhabitants of the world in love and charity, as is most certainly shown forth in the ninth section of the holy prophet, then I fear the Jews will reject Him; and, in fact, we are warned of that already in the third section of Jeremiah's word. To avoid this Israel must be taught that the prophecy of Isaiah does not stop with the Babylonian captivity and return to the kingdom of Heaven, and that Ezekiel's wheel do not whirl politically or spiritually in Heaven, but upon the earth, and have reference to earthly revolutions or changes, and show the bringing to pass of the great events of which this Babe of Bethlehem is the grandest of all.

Neither is the outlook of Daniel to be confined to the shade of the Maccabeean wall of Jewish conquest. Nor are these great questions to be decided by our unsuccessful attempts to find out what the prophet meant or what he might have understood himself to mean; but from the unity, totality, and organic connection of the whole body of prophecy, as referring to the kingdom of this world becoming subject to the Kingdom of the Saviour of all men. We, as Jews, are the only people that God has intrusted with the great questions, and, of course, the world will look to and expect us to give interpretation to these questions; and as we are intrusted with these things, God will hold us responsible if we fail to give the true light on the subject. Up to this time I am fearful the Jews as a nation are as much divided, and perhaps as much mistaken, as to the nature of His works, as other people. I find, by conversing with the Romans, Greeks, and others, that all their knowledge of these things of Jewish expectation of a Redeemer has been obtained from the Jews, either directly or indirectly, and it was through them Herod got the idea of his being a temporal King, and to rule and reign by the might of carnal weapons; whereas, if we consult the spiritual import of the prophets, his office is to blend all nations in one common brotherhood, and establish love in the place of law, and that heart should throb high with love to heart, and under this law a universal peace. Wherever one should meet another they should meet as friends; for what else can the prophet mean, in section nine, where he shows that this

King shall destroy all carnal weapons and convert them to a helpful purpose, and thus become the active worker in doing good to all men, and teaching all men to do good to each other?

By reading all the scrolls of God we find that the unity and totality of all the prophets go to bear us out in this idea, and all have reference to this Babe of Bethlehem. If we consult them as to the time, taking the revolutions of Ezekiel's wheel, they show plainly that the revolutions of the different governments of the world fix this as the time. Next, consult them in regard to the individuals connected with this great event. These are pointed to as the virgin wife, by Zacharias; next, the place has been pointed out and named; then the light and the appearing of the angels have all been set fourth, and also the opposition of the Romans has been declared. Now, I ask the High Court of the living God to look well on these things, and tell us how men that lived in different ages of the world, that lived in different portions of the country – men that never knew each other – men that were not prophesying for a party – men that had no personal interest in the subject as men – men that jeopardized, and some of them lost their lives on account of having uttered these prophecies – how could they all point out the place, the time, and the names of the parties so plain and clear, if it was not revealed to them and ordained by God Himself? I understand that the Romans and some of the priests have been saying that Zacharias was a hypocrite, and that Mary was a bad woman. Such might be the case, so far as a man is able to judge; but who, I ask, can forge such truth as these prophecies, and make them come true? Or who can cause light to decend from the Heavens and the angels come down and make the declaration that this was the Son of God, King of the Jews?

Noble Masters of the Sanhedrim, I was not alone. I am not the only witness of these things. The principle people of Bethlehem saw them and heard them as I did. I would say to you, if this is not the Jews' King, then we need not look for any other; for every line of prophecy has been most completely fulfilled in Him: and if He does not appear and save His own people I shall despair of ever being released, and I shall believe that we have misinterpreted the meaning of all the prophets. But I feel so sure that this is He I shall wait in expectation and with much anxiety, and I have no fears of any harm befalling Him. All the Romans in the world cannot harm Him; and although Herod may rage, may destroy all the infants in the world, the same angels that attended His birth will watch over Him through life, and the Romans will have to contend with the same God that Pharaoh did, and will meet with similar defeat.'"

Chapter 2

DURING THIS TIME, WHEN Jesus was about 26 years old, a representative of the Sanhedrim named Gamaliel interviewed His parents, a mentor and two of His close friends. Even the subject of marriage came up during these events. This interview was a real eye opener and a mind-altering revelation to behold.

Gamaliel's Interview

Gamaliel's Interview With JOSEPH And MARY
And OTHERS Concerning JESUS.

The *Hagiographa* or holy writings, found in the St. Sophia Mosque at Constantinople, made by Gamaliel, in the Talmuds of the Jews, 27 B. It seems Gamaliel was sent by the Sanhedrim to interrogate Joseph and Mary in regard to this child Jesus. He says:

" I found Joseph and Mary in the city of Mecca, in the land of Ammon or Moab. But I did not find Jesus. When I went to the place where I was told He was, He was somewhere else; and thus I followed Him from place to place, until I despaired of finding him at all. Whether He knew that I was in search of Him and did it to elude me, I cannot tell, though I think it most likely the former was the reason, for His mother says He is bashful and shuns company.

Joseph is a wood-working man. He is very tall and ugly. His hair looks as though it might have been dark auburn when young. His eyes are gray and vicious. He is anything but prepossessing in his appearance, and he is as gross and glum as he looks. He is a poor talker, and it seems that yes and no are the depth of his mind. I am satisfied he is very disagreeable to his family. His children look very much like him, and upon the whole I should call them a third-rate family. I asked him who were his parents. He said his father's name was Jacob, and his grandfather was Matthew. He did not like to talk on the subject. He is very jealous. I told him that we had heard that he had had

9

a vision, and I was sent to ascertain the facts in the case. He said he did not call it a vision; he called it a dream. He said after he and Mary had agreed to marry, it seemed that something told him that Mary was with child; that he did not know whether he was asleep or awake, but it made such an impression on his mind that he concluded to have nothing more to do with her; and while he was working one day under a shed, all at once a man in snow white stood by his side, and told him not to doubt the virtue of Mary, for she was holy before the Lord; that the child conceived in her was not by man, but by the Holy Ghost, and that the child would be free from human passions. In order to do this he must – that is, his humanity must – be of the extract of almah (that is the Hebrew word for virgin), that he might endure all things, and resist, and fill the demands of prophecy. He said the angel told him that this child should be great and should rule all the kingdoms of this world. He said that this child should set up a New Kingdom, wherein should dwell righteousness and peace, and that the kingdoms of this world which should oppose Him God would utterly destroy. I asked him, 'How could a virgin conceive of herself without the germination of a male?' He said: "This is the work of God. He has brought to life the womb of Elizabeth, so she had conceived and will bear a son in her old age who will go before and tell the people of this coming King." After telling me all these things, he disappeared like the melting down of a light. I then went and told Mary what had occurred, and she told me that the same angel, or one like him, had appeared to her and told the same things. So I married Mary, thinking that if what the angel had told us was true, it would be greatly to our advantage; but I am fearful we are mistaken. Jesus seems to take no interest in us, nor anything else much. I call him lazy and careless. I do not think he will ever amount to much, much less be a king. If he does, he must do a great deal better than he has been doing. I asked him how long after that interview with the angel before the child was born. He said he did not know, but he thought it was seven or eight months. I asked him where they were at the time. He said in Bethlehem. The Roman commander had given orders for all the Jews to go on a certain day to be enrolled as tax payers, and he and Mary went to Bethlehem as the nearest place of enrollment; and while there this babe was born. I asked if anything strange occurred there that night. He said that the people were much excited, but he was so tired that he had gone to sleep, and saw nothing. He said toward day there were several priests came in to see them and the babe, and gave them many presents. And the news got circulated that this child was to be King of the Jews, and it created such an excitement that he took the child and his mother and came to Moab for protection, for fear the Romans would kill the child to keep it from being a rival to the Romans.

I discovered that all Joseph's ideas were of a selfish kind. All he thought of was himself. Mary is altogether a different character, and she is too noble to be the wife of such a man. She seems to be about forty or forty-five years of age, abounds with a cheerful and happy spirit and is full of happy fancies. She is fair to see, rather fleshy, has soft and innocent-looking eyes, and seems to be naturally a good woman. I asked her who her parents were, and she said her father's name was Eli, and her mother's name was Anna; her grandmother's name was Pennel, a widow of the tribe of Asher, of great renown. I asked her if Jesus was the son of Joseph. She said he was not. I asked her to relate the circumstances of the child's history. She said that one day while she was grinding some meal there appeared at the door a stranger in shining raiment, which showed as bright as the light. She was very much alarmed at his presence, and trembled like a leaf; but all her fears were calmed when he spoke to her; for he said: 'Mary, thou art loved by the Lord and He has sent me to tell thee that thou shalt have a child; that this child shall be great and rule all nations of the earth.' She continued: 'I immediately thought of my engagement to Joseph, and supposed that was the way the child was to come; but he astonished me the more when he told me that cousin Elisabeth had conceived and would bear a son, whose name was to be John; and my son should be called Jesus. This caused me to remember that Zacharias had seen a vision and disputed with the angel, and for that he was struck with dumbness, so that he could no longer hold the priest's office. I asked the messenger if Joseph knew anything of the matter. He said that he told Joseph that I was to have a child by command of the Holy Ghost, and that he was to redeem his people from their sins, and was to reign over the whole world; that every man should confess to him and he should rule over all the kings of the earth.'

I asked her how she knew that he was an angel, and she said he told her so, and then she knew he was an angel from the way he came and went. I asked her to describe how he went away from her, and she said that he seemed to melt away like the extinguishing of a light. I asked her if she knew anything of John the Baptist. She said he lived in the mountains of Judea the last she knew of him. I asked her if he and Jesus were acquainted, or did they visit. She said she did not think they knew each other.

I asked her if at the time this angel, as she called him, visited her, she was almah (that is, virgin). She said she was; that she had never showed to man, nor was known by any man. I asked her if she at that time maintained her fourchette; and after making her and Joseph understand what I meant, they both said she had, and Joseph said this was the way he had of testing her virtue. I asked her if she knew when conception took place. She said she did not. I asked her if she was in any pain in bearing, or in delivering this child. She said, "None of any consequence." I asked her if he was healthy; to give me a description of his life. She said he was perfectly healthy; that she never heard him complain of any pain or dissatisfaction; his food always agreed with him; that he would eat anything set before him, and if anyone else complained he would often say he thought it good enough, much better than we deserved. She said that Joseph was a little hard to please, but this boy had answered him so often, and his answers were so mild and yet so suitable, that he had almost broken him of finding fault. She said he settled all the disputes of the family; that no odds what was the subject or who it was, one word from him closed all mouths, and what gave him such power was his words were always unpretending and spoken as though they were not intended as a rebuke, but merely as a decision. I asked her if she had ever seen him angry or out of humor. She said she had seen him apparently vexed and grieved at the disputes and follies of others, but had never seen him angry. I asked her if he had any worldly aspirations after money or wealth, or a great name, or did he delight in fine dress, like the most of youth. She said that was one thing that vexed her, he seemed to take no care of his person; he did not care whether he was dressed or not, or whether the family got along well or ill; it was all alike to Him. She said she talked to Him about it, and he would look at her a little grieved and say, 'Woman (for such He always called me), you do not know who I am.' Indeed, she said He takes so little interest in the things of the world and the great questions of the day, they were beginning to despair of His ever amounting to much – much less be a king, as the angel said He would be; if so, He would have to act very differently from what He was acting at the time. I told her that the Jewish doctors contend that the amorous disposition is peculiar to the male. I asked her if she had ever seen in the private life of Jesus any signs of such disposition. She said she had not. I asked if she saw in Him any particular fondness for female society. She said she had not; if anything, rather the contrary; that the young bethaul (the word in the Hebrew for young women) were very fond of Him, and were always seeking His society, and yet He seemed to care nothing for them; and if they appeared too fond of Him, He treated them almost with scorn. He will often get up and leave them, and wander away and spend His time in meditation and prayer. He is a perfect ascetic in His life. 'When I see how the people like to be with Him, and ask Him questions, and seem to take such delight with His answers – both men and women – it almost vexes me. They say there is a young woman in Bethany whom He intends to marry; but unless He changes His course very much He will never be qualified to have a family. But I do not believe the report. He never seems to me to care anything about women when He is in my presence.'

Thus it seems that Joseph and Mary have both lost all confidence in His becoming anything. They seem to think that the Sanhedrim should do something for Him to get Him out and let Him show Himself to the people. I tried to console them by telling them that my understanding of the prophecy was that He had to come to the high priesthood first, and there work in the spiritual domain of the heart; and when He had brought about a unity of heart and oneness of aim, it would be easy enough to establish His political claim; and all who would not willingly submit to Him, it would be an easy matter with the sword of Joshua or Gideon to bring under His control. It seems to me that His parents' ideas are of a selfish character; that they care nothing about the Jewish government nor the Romans oppression. All they think of is self-exaltation, and to be personally benefited by their son's greatness. But I told them they were mistaken; that the building up of the Kingdom of Heaven was not to be done by might nor by power, but by the Spirit of the Lord, and it would not do for us to use carnal weapons, nor to expect carnal pleasures to be derived therefrom; that it was not my understanding of the prophecy that this King was to use such weapons either for Himself or for the benefit of a party, but for the good of all men; that His dominion was to be universal, and it was to be of a spiritual character; that He was sent to the lost and not to the found.

His parents told me of an old man who lived on the road to Bethany who had once been a priest, a man of great learning, and well skilled in the laws and prophets, and that Jesus was often there with him reading the law and prophets together; that his name was Massalian, and that I might find Jesus there. But He was not there. Massalian said He was often at Bethany with a young family, and he thought there was some love affair between Him and one of the girls. I asked him if he had seen anything like a courtship between them. He said he had not, but inferred from their intimacy and from the fondness on the woman's part, as well as from the laws of nature, that such would be the case. I asked him to give me an outline of the character of Jesus. He said that He was a young man of the finest thought and feeling he ever saw in his life; that He was the most apt in His answers and solutions of difficult problems of any man His age he had ever seen; that His answers seem to give more universal satisfaction – so much so that the oldest philosopher would not dispute with Him, or in any manner join issue with Him, or ask the second time. I asked Massalian who taught Him to read and interpret the law and the prophets. He said that His mother said that He had always known how to read the law; that His mind seemed to master it from the beginning; and into the laws of nature and the relation of man to his fellow in His teachings or talks, He gives a deeper insight, inspiring mutual love and strengthening the common trust of society. Another plan He has of setting men right with the laws of nature: He turns nature into a great law book of illustrations, showing that every bush is a flame, every rock a fountain of water, every star a pillar of fire, and every cloud the one that leads to God. He makes nature preach the doctrine of trust in the divine Fatherhood. He speaks of the lilies as pledges from God's care and points to the fowls as evidence of His watchfulness over human affairs.

Who can measure the distance between God and the flower of the field? What connection is there between man and the lily? By such illustrations He creates a solicitude in man that seems to awe him into reverence, and he becomes attracted toward Heavenly thought, and feels that he is in the presence of One that is superior. In this talk He brings one to feel he is very near the presence of God. He says how much more your Father. The plan is one, though the intermediate points are immeasurably distant. Thus by beginning with a flower He reasons upward to the absolute, and then descends and teaches lessons of trust in a loving Father. The lessons of trust in God reassure the anxious listener and create an appetite that makes him long for more; and it often seems, when He has brought His hearers to the highest point of anxiety, He suddenly breaks off and leaves His company as though He cares nothing for them. Jesus in His talk brings all these illustrations to make man feel his nearness to his kindred, man, teaching also their relation to and dependence upon God; and although His method is happy, it does not seem to me that it is the most successful. He teaches that man and the flowers and birds drink from the same fountain and are fed from the same table, yet at the same time He seems to do everything to excite suspicion and prejudice. We that are watching Him to see His divine mission commence, He is continually tantalizing our expectations, as well as mocking our natural reason and desires. When a man separates himself from all other men, both in point of doctrine as well as discipline, he takes a great risk on his part – especially when he confines God to one channel, and that one of His own dictation. A man that assumes these responsible positions must have vast resources from which to draw, or he will sink in the whirlpool which his own impertinence has created. Through Jesus, in His teachings or talks (His words sound so much like the teachings of Hillel or Shammai that I must call it teaching, though He has no special scholars), we learn that God is Spirit, and God is Father; and He says these are the only two things that are essential for man to know. Then He illustrates this to the parents, and asks them what would they do for their children. He was telling some mothers a circumstances of a mother starving herself to feed her child, and then applied it to God as our Father; and they commenced shouting, they were so happy; and Jesus got up and left the house in seeming disgust.

Massalian says he is tempted at times to become impatient with Jesus, as He devotes so much time to details. It seems almost a waste of time for a man who came to save the world to be lingering over a special case of disease. He thinks he could hasten Jesus's physical deportment. Why not speak one word and remove every sick patient from his sick – bed at the same hour? What a triumph this would be. I asked him if Jesus had healed anyone. He said not as yet; but if He is to be King of the Jews, He was to heal all nations, and why not do it at once? If He would, there would be nothing more required to establish His kingship. But I said to him, 'Is it not equally so with God's creative power? See what time and labor it takes to bring forth a grain of corn. Why not have caused the earth to bring forth every month instead of every year? Christ was talking in defense of His Father. The people must learn to love and obey the Father before they would reverence the Son. Yes, he said the God that Jesus represented was One that the people might love and venerate; that He was a God of love, and had no bloody designs to execute on even a bad man, provided he ceased his evil ways.'

It is to be noted that in all Jesus's talk there are manifest references to the future. Many of His statements were like a sealed letter – not to be opened but by time. A grain of mustard was to result in a large tree. All His ideas refer to the future; like the parent helping the child with his burden of to-day, by telling of the blessings of tomorrow; and by making to-day the seed-corn of tomorrow; keeping the action of to-day under moral control by making the morrow the day of judgment. He stated futher that Jesus was a young man who was the best judge of human nature he had ever seen; that He thought at times He could tell men their thoughts and expose their bad principles; and while He and all these advantages of life, He seemed not to care for them nor to use them abusively. He seems to like all men – one as well as another – so much so that His own parents have become disgusted with Him, and have almost cast Him off. But Jesus has such a peculiar temperament that He seems not to care, and is as well satisfied with one as another. He said that Jesus seemed fond of Mary and Martha, who lived at Bethany, and probably I might find Him there.

Massalian is a man of very deep thought and most profound judgment. All his life he has made the Scriptures his study. He, too, is a good judge of human nature, and he is satisfied that Jesus is the Christ. He said that Jesus seemed to understand the prophecy by intuition. I asked him where Jesus was taught to read the prophecy. He said that His mother told him that Jesus could read from the beginning; that no one ever taught Him to read. He said that he, in making quotations from the prophets, was sometimes mistaken or his memory failed him; but Jesus could correct him every time without the scroll; and that sometimes he thought Jesus was certainly mistaken, but never in a single instance was He wrong. I asked him to describe His person to me, so that I might know Him if I should meet Him. He said: 'If you ever meet Him you will know Him. While He is nothing but a man, there is something about Him that distinguishes Him from every other man. He is the picture of His mother, only He has not her smooth, round face. His hair is a little more golden than hers, though it is as much from sunburn as anything else. He is tall, and His shoulders are a little drooped; His visage is thin and of a swarthy complexion, though this is from exposure. His eyes are large and a soft blue, and rather dull and heavy. The lashes are long, and his eyebrows are very large. His nose is that of a Jew. In fact, He reminds me of an old-fashioned Jew in every sense of the word. He is not a great talker, unless there is something brought up about Heaven and divine things, when His tongue moves glibly and His eyes light up with a peculiar brilliancy; though there is this peculiarity about Jesus, He never argues a question; He never disputes. He will commence and state facts, and they are on such a solid basis that nobody will have the boldness to dispute with Him. Though He has such mastership of judgement, He takes no pride in confuting His opponents, but always seems to be sorry for them. I have seen Him attacked by the scribes and doctors of the law, and they seemed like little children learning their lessons under a master. His strongest points are in the spiritual power of the law and the intentions of the prophets. The young people tried to get Him to take a class of them and teach them; but He utterly refused.' This Jew is convinced that He is the Messiah of the world.

I went from there to Bethany, but Jesus was not there. They said He and Lazarus were away, they could not tell where. I went and saw Mary and Martha, the sisters of Lazarus, and had a long talk with them. They are very pleasant and nice young maids, and Mary is quite handsome. I teased her about Jesus, but they both denied that Jesus was anything like a lover; He was only a friend; though this is so common for young maids I did not know whether to believe them or not until I told them my real business. And when I told them that this was the same person that was born to the virgin in

Bethlehem some twenty-six years before, and that His mother had told me all the facts in the case, they seemed deeply interested. They then told me upon their honor that Jesus never talked or even hinted to either one of them on the subject of marriage. Martha blushed, and said she wished He had. If He was to be king, she would like to be queen. I asked them if they had ever seen Him in the company of young virgins. They said they had not. I asked them if they had heard Him talk about young girls, or if He sought their society more than that of men; and they both declared they had not; and they were very much surprised that He did not. I asked them what He talked of when in their company; and they said He was not much in their company; that He and their brother would go upon the house-top and stay there half the night, and sometimes all night, talking and arguing points of interest to them both. Mary said she had often gone near, so she could listen to them, for she had often gone near, so she could listen to them, for she loved to hear Him talk, He was so mild and unpretending, and then was so intelligent that He was different from any and all other young men she had ever seen. I asked them what was their brother's opinion of Him. They said he thought there never was such a man on earth. He thought Him to be one of God's prophets. He said when they are out in the mountains, as they are most of the time, Jesus can tell him about the flowers, trees, and rocks, can tell him everything in the world, and that none of the wild animals are afraid of Him. He says often the stag and the wolf will come and stand for Jesus to stroke their mane, and seem almost loath to go away from Him. He says that no poisonous serpent will offer to hiss at Him. Their brother thinks He is perfectly safe if Jesus is with him. I asked them if He had ever told their brother anything about Himself. They said that if He had spoken to their brother He had not told them.

"Now, Masters of Israel, after having investigated this matter; after tracing Jesus from His conception to the present time; after obtaining all the information that is to be had on this important subject, getting it from those who are more likely to tell the truth from the fact they are disinterested persons; and then taking a prophetical as well as a historical view of the subject, I have come to the conclusion that this is the Christ that we are looking for. And as a reason for my conclusion, I will call your attention to the following facts: First to the prophecy of Isaiah, section 7: 'And he said, Hear now, saith the Lord. Oh, house of David, is it a small thing for you? Therefore the Lord Himself shall give you a sign; behold, a virgin shall conceive and bear a son, and shall call His name God with men. Butter and honey shall He eat, that He may know to refuse the evil and choose the good; for before the child shall know to refuse the evil and choose the good the land that God abhorrest shall be forsaken of her king.' Section 8: 'Bind the testimony; seal the law among His disciples; the Lord will hide His face from the house of Jacob, and he will look for Him.' Here is a literal fulfillment of this word of the Most High God, so clear and plain that none may mistake. Jeremiah, 31st section: 'Turn, oh virgin, to thy people, for the hand of the Lord is upon thee; for the Lord shall create a new thing in the earth; a woman shall compass a man.' Here again are set forth the same things that Isaiah speaks of and the same things that I have learned from Mary. Micah, section 5: 'Thou, Bethlehem Ephratah, thou art little among the thousands of Judah; out of thee shall come forth unto Me Him that shall rule My people. He is from everlasting; and I will give them up until the time she travaileth to bring forth My first born, that He may rule all people.' Here we have the city, the virgin, the office, His manner of life, the seeking Him by the Sanhedrim. All these things are under our eyes as full and complete as I now write them, who have all this testimony given in this letter. How can we as a people dispute these things? In the 49th section of Genesis, making reference to the history, that is now upon us, the writer says: 'A captive shall not depart from Judah, nor a lawmaker from him, until Shiloh come, and gather His people between His feet, and keep them forever."

Chapter 3

Some times people in controlling positions will do actions that most laymen may think are unjust or even a cover for a deception to the real motive of their actions. How many of us have seen these kinds of action first hand, to know in your heart that some one is lying in order to keep themselves in a more considerable light. But in their minds as to what they are saying that others should believe, they use the letter of the law to get away with "murder" when we may know that its only a twist of words to their benefit that are being used.

Here is found a very interesting take on a subject that we have all heard of but did not know the reasoning behind the actions taken. Remember, that there are times when its been determined in everlasting times past that a certain person will be put into position in future times to come in order to carry out a deed that the person involved has no idea will happen years later after their birth. God knows what He is doing.

Report of CAIAPHAS to the SANHEDRIM Concerning

The Execution of JESUS.

Records of the Jerusalem Sanhedrim, By Eliezer Hyran, B. 24.
Taken in Constantinople, October 16, 1883

"Caiaphas, Priest of the Most High God, to the Masters of Israel, greeting:"
"In obedience to your demands for a reason for my action in the case of Jesus of Nazareth, and in defense of my conduct, I beg leave to submit the following for your consideration: I would assure you that it was not on account of personal malice, envy, or hate, that existed in my own nature, nor for the want of a willingness upon my part to conform to the Jewish law in its strictest sense. I had but very little personal knowledge of the Nazarene. The most I knew of this man was from outside sources. Nor was it because He claimed to be the King of the Jews, nor because He said He was the Son of God – I would that He were – nor because He prophesied or ignored the holy temple. No, nor all

of these combined. There is a cause, and a more weighty matter, back of all these things that controlled my action in the matter. Therefore, I hope you will investigate strictly on legal principles the reasons that I may give.

IN ORDER THAT YOU may be able to see and weigh the question fully, and remember the responsibility that rests on me according to the laws of our nation, I will ask you to go back with me to the chronicles of our history as a commonwealth. First, our faith is pledged to one living and true God, this God being indescribable, unchangeable, incomprehensible, and, of course, unnameable. But yet in our daily communications with, and our applications to Him, He has been pleased to give us His name, or His several names, according to His relations to us, and they are found nowhere, only in the ark of His holy temple – there where He presents to us His strength and power. He calls Himself Eloi, which means almighty in strength; that He can do what He will without effort; that He does the greatest thing as easy as He does the least. This makes Him different from all beings. In His Holy Ark He records Himself Elaah – existence without beginning, and no contingency as to His end. Again, He writes Himself Hhelejon – unchangeable; that is, nothing but His own will can change Him. Again, He records His name Jah – knowledge that comprehends without comprehended. Again He is written Adonia – full and free, and freely full. Combining the several names we have Jehovah – the Hebrew God. A man never can go wrong while he can pronounce this name in its comprehensive sense. This is where the Zealots, the Sadducees, and Essenes had their origin, and it is the want of being able to pronounce this name in its comprehensive sense that causes so much dissension among the Jews. Jesus could pronounce this name, but He stole it out of the temple, as I am creditably informed.

But the object I call your attention to is in pronouncing this name, with all its bearings, may be seen if we turn to the third Book of Leviticus, section 10, wherein is the special order made by our God to Moses, that we should offer the bullock, the ram, the flour and oil, and the people should fast seven days, and this should be kaphar, or atonement for the sins of all the people. Now, unless Moses was deceived, he has deceived us, or Jesus of Nazareth is a false teacher; for all He teaches is metanoeite, metanoeite, as though a man's being sorry for a crime would make restitution to the offended party. A man might repent ever so much, but what good would that do toward healing the man he had injured? None in the least. This mode of making atonement was ordained of God and revealed to Moses; but if man has nothing to do but to repent, the disease carries its own remedy with it. So a man can sin as often as he may wish to. Look at the first book, section 3: 'And God said to Abraham, by His own mouth, that each and all that were circumcised by the cutting of the prepuce should be saved.' This should be the seal of the covenant. Now, if this is not true, God must go against His own contract, violate His own promises, as well as deceive the faith and cheat the obedience of His own children. This is all so, if Jesus's teaching be true, for He sets up table (baptism) as the seal of God. I refer you to section 10, division first, where God said to Moses that He had changed the laws, converted the elements for the protection of His people, and with His own arm had delivered them out of a strong compact; and that they might remember, and that the generation to be born might remember and never forget to trust in Him when in danger, He said that once every year we should roast a kid or lamb, and eat it with unleavened bread, and this should be the sign that we would trust in Him in all times of danger. Now Jesus teaches that common bread and wine are to be used instead thereof – a thing unheard of. And not only so, something that is altogether repugnant to God, and something that fosters drunkenness, and is well qualified to excite men's passions. And oh, ye Masters of Israel, but think once. Jesus calls Himself the Son of God; claims to have been born of almah (the Hebrew word for virgin); that He and His Father are one – They are equal. These things will establish the following conclusions: If He is right, His Father is false. If They were one, then Their teachings would be one; and if His teachings are true, God's must be wrong, or there are not those perfections in Him that we learn in pronouncing His holy name. By tolerating the teachings of Jesus, we say to the Romans that all of our former teachings are false; that the Hebrew's God is not to be trusted; that He is weak, wanting in forethought; that He is vacillating and not to be trusted, much less to be honored and obeyed. Thus the world will lose confidence in our God, and confidence in us as a religious people. This is impregnating the whole atmosphere with moral pollution. It does not only cut off, but blocks the way of all Jews from heaven; and not only this, it excludes our hope in the salvation of our forefathers, who have obeyed God in His ordinances, believed in His promises, and shouted in the triumphs of a holy life for fourteen hundred years. He entirely ignores God's holy temple – the house God had built by our forefathers under His own supervision, where He promises to dwell with His children, to hear their prayers, and to be pleased with their sacrifices. This temple is the bond of the Jews. Here all men can come and be blessed. It is the earthly home of the souls of men – the place where men may hide from the storms of sin and persecution. This temple is where the foolish may learn wisdom, the place where the naked soul can be clothed, and where the hungry may be fed. This the grandest gift of our Father. Jesus completely ignores this temple; says the priests have made it a den of thieves; and sets up a sneer, and even scoffs at its sacred ordinances, and with a sort of selfish triumph says it shall be destroyed; and from His manner of saying it, I have no doubt He would be glad to see it quickly done. But what would be the condition of our people if this temple was removed? What would be the priesthood if the temple was destroyed? Where would we find an answer by Urim and Thummim? How would the soul of man be purified, if the holy Bathkole, the Euroch of God, should depart? There in that sacred temple of God he has been burning to the consuming of sin and the purifying of the heart since our return from bondage in Babylon. My argument is, if this temple is destroyed, or even forsaken by the Jews, we as a nation are utterly ruined. We might as well put our necks under the feet of idolatry and give up all hope.

One more subject I place before my Masters of Israel. Is it compatible with our religion, or is it consistent with philosophy, or admitted in His Holy Word, that there can be more gods than one? When we pronounce Ele Laah Shaddiai – Hhelyon Adonai (which is Jehovah), there can be but one living God. By reference to section 6, No. four, He says by mouth of Moses, when he was all aglow with glory of God – and remember He speaks either by mouth or quill; it is He that speaks, and not man – He says, 'The Lord your God is one God; there can be one. I am and have been with you; I brought you up; I delivered you out of a strong compact; I delivered you out of their hand and kept you dry, while your enemies were drowned in the sea. I will not forsake you. I promised your father I would not. But if you forsake Me, then desolation will come upon you, and have you in swift desolation.' In section 5, three and four of David's Song of Joy: 'I am God alone. If I turn to the right or to the left, if I go down into the depths of the sea, or into the centre of the earth, or ever the heavens, I should find no companion.' In section 3 He says: 'I am God alone, and alone I am God; besides me there is no help for man nor angels.' Then in section 13, this command has been given: 'Thou shall pay to the Lord thy God once a year a half-shekel of silver, that thou and thy children, and all the strangers that are within thy gate, may know that there is no God besides Me, on whom they may call in time of danger.' Now, having all these commandments and teachings from the very lips of God Himself before my eyes, and being held responsible for the soundness of our doctrine and the proper inculcation of the same among the people of the Jews, what was I to do? Could I stand as the priest of the Most High God, and see your blessed religion perverted by an imposter? Could I stand and see the holy temple of our God deserted and forsaken? Could I stand and see all the holy ordinances, which had been appointed by our God for securing salvation to Israel, perverted by an imposter? All the blessed doctrines that were appointed for the government and instruction of the priesthood, thence to be imparted to the youth of our land, set aside, and that by one that could show not only the authority of John the Baptist, who could give no authority of the one who sent him to baptize, and he could not tell who he was, nor whence he came? Hence you can see the responsible position that I as the high priest of God and of the Jewish Church occupied. According to our laws I was made responsible, and stood between God and my people, to protect them in doctrine and government. I refer you to the capitulation made by the Sanhedrim and Augustus Caesar, in the holy Tosephta of the Talmuds. We submitted to taxation by the Romans, and the Romans are to protect our holy religion from foreign foes, in order that the holy temple or any of its sacred ordinances should never be molested, nor the holy city, Jerusalem, be polluted by Roman idolatry. Now the insinuating plan adopted by Jesus was well qualified to deceive the common people. It had already led many to forsake the temple, and hold her ordinances in derision, as well as to neglect the teachings of the priest or to pay the tithes for their supplies. He had already inculcated into the Jewish mind his pernicious ways of being saved to the extent that the Jewish cause was almost lost. There are two reasons for this: First, the people to whom he preached were an ignorant set, and knew but very little about doctrine of any kind. They are a restless sort of men, who are always finding fault and wanting something new, and never associate with the more enlightened part of the community in order to learn. Another reason of his having many followers is, his doctrines are congenial to unsanctified flesh. They are so suited to human nature that they require no sacrifices; they need not go to the temple to worship God; they need not fast, and they can pray when and where they please; they need pay no tithes to keep up the temple or the priesthood, but every man can be his own priest and worship God as he chooses. All this is so compatible with human nature that, although he has not been preaching over three years, he has more followers to-day than Abraham has, and they have become perfectly hostile toward the Jews that are faithful to their God; and, if it had not been for the Roman soldiers, on the day of his execution we would have had one of the bloodiest insurrections ever known to the Jewish commonwealth. I am told that there was never seen such a concourse of people assembled at Jerusalem as at the cross. One of my guards informs me that there were several hundred thousand, and although there were two others crucified at the same time, Jesus was the great centre of attraction. They would call out, 'Who is this Jesus of Nazareth? What is his crime?' Some of his friends would cry out, 'Nothing; he is being executed because he was a friend to the poor.' 'Take him down! Take him down,' they would cry out, and the soldiers would have to use their spears to keep them back. But when he yielded up the ghost he proved to all that he was hypostatical (that is, a human body), and the lodi curios had come from the iclandic covenant, and his trinitatis unitas was all a sham, for how could this unpronounced name suffer or be captured by men, or die, unless he is the one that is to die for the many? And if so, I was only accomplishing God's holy purposes, which exonerates me from guilt.

But it seems to me a necessity that he should be removed. That this may be evident to your minds, I ask you to contrast our present condition with the pass. Jesus of Nazareth spent two years in Egypt under the instruction of Rabbi Joshua, and learned the art of thaumaturgy to perfection, as has never been taught in any of the schools of necromancy among the heathen. If the healing miracles of Jesus are true, as they must be (for they are so acknowledged by his foes as well as his friends), he must have learned it from Horus and Serapis, as practiced by those heathen priest. He came back to Palestine as a physician, and was by nature an enthusiast as well as a Hebrew patriarch, and when John's preaching excited idealistic minds, Jesus also went to that teacher, and was inspired by him to inculcate and promulgate his doctrines. Notwithstanding his youth and inexperience, Jesus started out as a public orator and teacher with the doctrines of John, and in that capacity referred exclusively to his authority, as every public teacher in these days has to be ordained by some acknowledged authority. As long as John was at large, Jesus in the capacity of an itinerant teacher and physician roused the people of Galilee to metanoia (repentance of sin), to bring about a restoration of the kingdom of heaven. He met with the same opposition that John did from those who would not admit that they were more sinful than their progenitors were, or that asceticism was the proper means for the restoration of the kingdom of heaven. But he met with the same success among the lower classes, such as foreign harlots, Sodomites, publicans, and other Roman agents, But the intelligent portion remained cold and unmoved by his enthusiasm. The cures which he performed appeared miraculous to his followers, but most ridiculous to the intelligent Jews and men of sober and reflective minds.

Jesus embraced the humanitarian doctrine of the Hillelites, presenting conspicuously cosmopolitan spirit of Judaism, and he did it almost in the words of Hillel, who had taught it before. Their faith and doctrine being alike, it was not hard for him to create excitement, or to find plenty of followers. In addition to all this, he taught a system of low morals, and so void of all ritualistic ideas that it was easy for him to get any number of followers. He taught the people that there was but one living and true God, but he taught them that he was that God, and that his Father was merged into himself, and could manifest himself only through him, which theory would confute itself if they would only stop to reflect, for as he was hypostatical or corporeal, his assistance was cut off from all that was not immediately in his presence, which is altogether incompatible with the faith of the Jews. Right in the face of this doctrine he would teach that there was a special providence, as well as a general providence, as if there could be a general providence without a God that could be present in all times, as we learn in pronouncing His name. He taught that the dead will rise and live again in a future state of happiness or misery according as they have lived here. Therefore he taught future rewards and punishments; but he being present, how could he reward in the future? He taught the revelation on the prophets, but contradicted all they teach. He taught the election of Israel by the Almighty, but ignored all the doctrines of Israel. He taught the eternity of God's laws, and promises in the super-importance of humanitarian over the ritual laws and doctrines, but I do not think he wishes to abolish the latter, or even the traditional laws, but merely to supersede them by a higher life. The natural result of all this was that he disregarded the laws of Levitical cleanness, which were considered so important by the Shammaites and Essenes, and also by the Hillelites. This is the point where division commenced, and the breach grew wider and wider until an insurrection must have been the result. He so far cut himself loose from the Jews that he ate with unclean sinners, publicans, and lepers, and permitted harlots to touch him, while his disciples went so far as to eat their meals without washing themselves. Furthermore, he looked upon the whole of the Levitical institutions, temples, sacrifices, and priesthood included, as no longer necessary and not worth the life of an animal. This was certainly the opinion of the Hillelites. Jesus, it seems, found in this Hillelite School a party furnished to hand, ready to take up with his heresy (and a large party they are, almost sufficient to divide the whole Jewish commonwealth). They taught the repentance of sin, the practicing of benevolence and charity, the education of the young, and good-will toward mankind, as possessing much more moral worth than all the Levitical cleanness, or compliance with the whole moral law given to us by our God to govern us. His preaching was of the parabolic style. He would rely on a text of scripture, for he seemed to hold the scriptures in high veneration, so his preaching was on the midrash style of the scribes – a maxim expressed in the style of Solon or Sirach's son. His great object was to come as near the Jewish theology as possible so as to destroy the Jews' entirely, and establish his own. Hence he resorted to the allegorical method of the Egyptian Hebrews, uttering many good and wise sayings, which were not new to the learned, but which were taken from the common wisdom of the country, which was known by all who were acquainted with the literature of the rabbis. But they were new to his class of hearers, who were not accustomed to listening to the wise. He had no education, comparatively speaking. He was full of nervous excitement, all of which went to inspire his hears with enthusiasm. He took but little care of his health or person; cared not for his own relatives. He traveled mostly on foot in the company of his disciples and some suspicious women, and lived on the charity of his friends. He seemed to take no notice of the political affairs of his country; would as soon be governed by one nation as another. In fact, it seemed if he had any preference it was for the Romans. It seemed that he became so infatuated that he really thought he was the head of the Kingdom of Heaven. This manner of preaching, along with his presumption, aroused his enemies to a powerful pitch, and it was all I could do to keep the zealots from mobbing him in the temple. They had no confidence in a doctrine that set the Jewish laws at naught, and mocked the priesthood of God, and they with the Sadducees and scribes were not willing to submit to a man who acknowledged no authority higher than himself, and was seemingly endeavoring to overturn everything that they held more sacred and dearer than life. Jesus's mode and manner were well qualified to deceive the unsuspecting. 'Let us have all things in common.' Said he, 'and he that would be greatest among you will prove his greatness by rendering the greatest service to all, and if any of the higher powers compel the to go a mile, let him that is compelled go ten miles.' This caused him to be attacked more in his policy than in his doctrine. The great question with us Jews was, here are the Romans upon us; how can we get rid of them? Jesus's idea was to let the Romans alone; it matters not who rules and governs the nations; if they abuse you, love them in return, and they cannot be your enemies long; no man can continue to abuse another who returns injuries with love. Keep from them; pray in secret for the return of the Kingdom of Heaven and God's grace, and this will soon make all things right. 'pay your taxes,' he would say to them; 'it is only Caesar's money you pay, which is unlawful for you to have – unlawful on account of its idolatrous effigies.' Again, he would say to his hearers, 'You cannot conquer the Romans; better convert them, and they are your enemies no longer. They already have your temple in their possession; their yoke is getting heavier everyday, and the more you fight against them the more they will abuse you; therefore, your only chance is to love them, and try to make your yoke easy and your burden light by having them your friends.' Indeed, the conduct of Jesus was so strange and incompatible with the interest of the Jews as a nation, that it seemed to me that he was a subject employed by the Romans to keep the Jews submissive and obedient to all their tyranny and abuse.

This policy was most powerfully attacked by the officiating priest, by the Shammaites and Zealots, and, in fact, the whole Jewish nation was becoming aroused to a war heat. The reprimands of Jesus were so severe against the rich and highly educated that they had turned against him, and brought all the power they had, both of their wealth and talent, so that I saw that a bloody insurrection was brewing fast. The public mind of the Jews was becoming more and more divided and corrupt; heretical doctrines were being diffused all over the land; the temple was forsaken and the holy sacraments neglected; the people were dividing into sects, and these breaches were like a rent in a garment – tearing wider apart continually. As it seemed to me, the whole of the Jewish theocracy was about to be blown away as a bubble on a breaker.

As the Jews became more and more divided and confused, the tyranny of the Romans increased. All they wanted was an excuse to slaughter the Jews and confiscate their property. At this time both the doctrine and religion of the Jews were spreading rapidly all over Rome, which gave the Romans great alarm. Sejane undertook to have an ordinance passed in the Senate, abolishing the Jewish religion from Rome; and when he found it would cause an insurrection, they banished all the Jews from Rome, and back they came to Judea with all their idolatry and heresy, and many other corrupt principles from the Romans, which fitted them to join any party for profit. Up to this time the Romans governors had shown great kindness to the Jews. There never was a better man than Hyrcan. The Jews enjoyed great peace during his administration. But Tiberias has turned against us; Pilate has removed the army from Caesarea to Jerusalem. I say, no nation with any self-respect, or one that had any energy left, would or could stand it without a struggle.

Now, the preaching of John the Baptist and Jesus of Nazareth had brought all these things upon us. When Herod Antipas captured John, it quieted matters in Galilee, so that they had peace until Jesus started it up afresh. I had issued orders to Jesus to desist from preaching, unless he taught as the Jews taught. He sent me the impertinent word that his doctrine was not of this world, but had reference to the world to come; when he was all the time doing all he could to destroy the peace and harmony of this world. Now, according to our law in the Saphra, by Jose. B. Talmud, it devolves on me to see that the people have sound doctrine taught them. Hence it is my duty to examine all the midrashim, or sermons, of all the preaching priests, and if anyone teach the people wrongly, or if his conduct is not in correspondence with his profession, to cause him to desist; or if any disregard the holy laws of ablution, or in any way defile himself, or if he shall be guilty of misconduct in any way, either in manner of life or doctrine, to adjudge such a one, and pronounce sentence for his crime upon him. This I did upon

Jesus of Nazareth, to save the church from heresy, and to save the cause of the Jewish commonwealth from final ruin. But understand that I did not act rashly nor illegally, as I am accused. I only passed sentence under the protest and order of the whole court belonging to the high priest, containing twelve members, or elders, and priest. Thus you will see it was not my voluntary act, but was a legal one and in accordance with law. After I examined Jesus on the various charges, he said in the presence of all the court that each and all of them were true. I then reasoned with him, and asked him, if the court of high priest would forgive him of these charges would he desist from these things in all time to come. He answered most emphatically and positively he would not. Under these circumstances I was compelled, according to our law, to sentence him to die; for if he continued to promulgate his pernicious heresies the Jews, as a nation, must perish with their religion. And, as you find in the Toseppta, that the nation has always the right of self-preservation, and as we had conceded the right to the Romans of executing our criminal laws, it became my painful duty to send him to Pontius Pilate, with the following charges:

" 'Caiaphas, High Priest of the Most High God,
to Pontius Pilate, Governor of the Roman Province.' "

Jesus of Nazareth is thus charged by the High Court of the Jews:

First, with teaching the doctrine that there are more gods than one, which is contrary to the teachings of the Jewish law, which he most positively refuses to desist from in the presence of this court.

Second, he teaches that he is a God, which is contrary to the Jewish law, and he is visible and comprehensible; and, after being asked to desist by this court, he most positively affirms that he is the Son of God.

Third, he teaches and affirms that the Bath kole (Holy Spirit) cannot come until he goes away, which is contrary to the teachings of the Jews; because it was He that brooded over the waters, and has been in the habitual light of the world ever since; from all of which he refuses to desist.

He teaches baptism as the seal of God, instead of circumcision, which was established by the decrees of God with Abraham as a seal of the Jews; and when adjured to desist by this court declared he would not.

He teaches asceticism as the means of salvation, contrary to the Jewish custom; and affirmed in the presence of this court he would not desist.

He teaches that the Levitical ablution is of no service, while we hold that the outward washing is the sign of inward purity; and when adjured to desist he emphatically refused.

He has abrogated the ordinances given by God to Moses of the pascal supper, wherein we should roast a lamb and eat it with unleavened bread; but Jesus has introduced a custom altogether different - without any authority. He has introduced common bread and wine, which are not only forbidden, but are well qualified to excite men's passions and make them forget God rather than to remember and trust Him, this feast having been introduced that we should remember to trust Him in the hours of trouble. When asked why he did this, all He would say was: "Hitherto I work, and my Father works."

He has abrogated the priesthood, and set the temple at naught, which is the very life's blood of the Jewish faith.

Were it not that God our Father has given us these holy ordinances we would not be so tenacious of them. We know they are the pillars upon which the Jewish theocracy is built, and that we cannot live without them. Although Jesus of Nazareth has been adjured time and again to stop teaching these ways of death, he has as often declared he would not; therefore it devolves on me as the proper and the only officer to pronounce sentence upon him."

These charges were written by my scribe, and sent with the officers to Pilate for his consent. Of course, I did not expect him to execute Him as he did, but it seems that the mob was so great that Pilate never received them. I expected Pilate to send Jesus back to me, so that I could send him to you for your approval; and if so, then I would proceed to try him with Urim and Thummim, with the regular lacktees on guard, as our law requires; but it seems that Pilate thirsted for his blood. Like all guilty tyrants, he was afraid of his own shadow, and wished to destroy everything that threatened his power.

With these reasons for my actions, I submit the case which I am sure will be considered favorably by my Masters of Israel."

Chapter 4

Report of CAIAPHAS to the SANHEDRIM
Concerning the Resurrection of JESUS

APPROXIMATELY THE FOLLOWING WEEK or so after Caiaphas' report to Pilate and then to the Sanhedrim, he had his scribe pen another report to the Sanhedrim about the circumstances surrounding the resurrection of Jesus.

Before sharing it with you, I would like to show you some descriptions that explains dimensions and origins of some of the materials used during those days.

First, after the proceeding report was translated and continuing to unwind futher into the scroll, another report was found that was written by him. A scroll is similar to a parchment. A scroll is made from what is known in the Hebrew tongue as numet, which is a word that means "pulp", made from the bark of the reed into a paste, dried in the sun until it is hard; when pressed and polished it shines beautifully, and compared to our paper, it is just as smooth. There are two kinds or types used: papyrus, and the more expensive, hierotike, which is used by the priest alone. It is approximately sixteen inches wide, and is cemented together by a gum that exudes from a tree that resembles the Elm tree. Fashioned like our pens, the common reed quill is what was used to write upon these scrolls by the sopher, which is Hebrew for scribe. In the Greek, he's called a grammateus. The reports were written in what is known as square Hebrew. With letters ranging from a half-inch to an inch in size, you can imagine the amount and size of a roll of parchment it would take to record a deed during those times. Even the best Hebrew scholars have difficulties reading them, and must have textbooks to assist them. But after getting the gist of the subject, they are able to make it through it OK.

The windlass, as it may be called is a square piece of timber, about three inches in diameter, to which the scroll is fastened at one end, around which it is rolled like a spool. At the proper distance are tied two transverse sticks to hold the parchment to its proper place. The windlass with the scroll is placed at one end of a table, and an empty windlass at the other end, so that as you unwind from the one to read, the scroll winds around the other. The letters are very distinct with hundreds of them arranged in rows. All are numbered and lettered with the dates on them, making it easy to find anything they desire to read. Another class of books of fine sheep or goatskin is about eight by twelve inches dimensionally, with very fine writing that is difficult to read. These books are bound between cedar boards with clasps and contain from eight to forty sheets. Josephus wrote seventy-two of these types of books.

These scrolls can be found in Constantinople in the mosque of St. Sophia, preserved at Mohammed's order. It is written as follows:

Sanhedrim, 89. By Siphri II, 7.:

" To You, Masters of Israel:

As I have made a former defense to you, and you have approved the same, I feel in duty bound to communicate to you some facts that have come to my knowledge since that communication. A few days after the execution of Jesus of Nazareth the report of his resurrection from the dead became so common that I found it necessary to investigate it, because the excitement was more intense than before, and my own life as well as that of Pilate was in danger. I sent for Malkus, the captain of the royal city guard, who informed me he knew nothing personally, as he had placed Isham in command of the guard; but from what he could learn from the soldiers the scene was awe-inspiring, and the report was so generally believed that it was useless to deny it. He thought my only chance was to suppress it among the soldiers, and have John and Peter banished to Crete, or arrested and imprisoned, and if they would not be quiet, to treat them as I had treated Jesus. He said that all the soldiers had conversed with were convinced that Jesus was resurrected by supernatural power and was still living, and that he was no human being, for the light and the angels and the dead that came out of their graves all went to prove that something had happened that never occurred on earth before. He said that John and Peter were spreading it all over the country, and that if Jesus would appear at the head of a Host, and declare for the King of the Jews, he believed all the Jews would fight for Him. I sent for the lieutenant, who gave a lengthy account of the occurrence that morning, all of which I supposed you have learned, and will investigate. From this I am convinced that something transcending the laws of nature took place that morning, that cannot be accounted for upon natural laws, and I find it useless to try to get any of the soldiers to deny it, for they are so excited that they cannot be reasoned with. I regret that I had the soldiers placed at the tomb, for the very things that they were to prevent they have helped to establish.

After questioning the soldiers and officers to my satisfaction, my mind being so disturbed that I could neither eat nor sleep, I sent for John and Peter. They came and brought Mary and Joanna, who are the women that went to embalm Jesus" body the morning of the resurrection, as it is called. They were very interesting as they related the circumstances. Mary says that when they went day was just breaking. They met the soldiers returning from the sepulchre, and saw nothing strange until they came to the tomb, and found that it was empty. The stone that covered the sepulchre was rolled to one side, and two men dressed in flowing white were sitting, one at each end of the sepulchre. Mary asked them where was her Lord; they said, 'He is risen from the dead; did He not tell you He would rise the third day and show Himself to the people, to prove that He was the Lord of life?' Go tell His disciples, said they. Joanna said she saw but one man; but this discrepancy must have been due to their excitement, because they say they were much alarmed. They both say that as they return they met the Master, who told them that He was the Resurrection and the Life; all that will accept shall be resurrected from the second death. 'We fell at His feet, all bathed in tears, and when we rose up He was gone.' Both these women wept for joy while relating these circumstances, and John shouted aloud, which made me tremble in every limb, for I could not help thinking that something that was the exclusive work of God had occurred, but what it all meant was a great mystery to me. It might be, I said, that God had sent this message by the mouth of this stranger; it might be that He was the seed of the woman, and we His people had executed Him.

I asked John and Peter if they could give me any further evidence in regard to this man; that I wished to be informed of His private history. Peter said that Jesus passed by where he was, and bade him to follow Him, and he felt attracted to Him, but at first it was more through curiosity than anything in the man; that he soon became acquainted with Mary, who told him that He was her son, and related to him the strange circumstances of His birth, and that she was convinced that He was to be the king of the Jews. She spoke of many strange things concerning His life, which made Peter feel more interested in Him than he would have been otherwise. He said that Jesus was a man so pleasant in His character, and so like a child in innocence, that no one could help liking Him after he got acquainted with Him; that though He seemed to be stern and cold, He was not so in reality; that He was exceedingly kind, especially to the poor; that He would make any sacrifice for the sick and needy, and would spare no effort to impart knowledge to anyone that would call on Him, and that His knowledge was so profound that he had seen Him interrogated by the most learned doctors of the law, and He always gave the most perfect satisfaction, and that the sopher or scribes, and the Hillelites, and Shammaites were afraid to open their mouths in His presence. They had attacked Him so often and had been repelled that they shunned Him as they would a wolf; but when He had repelled them He did not enjoy the triumph as they did over others of whom they had gotten the ascendancy. As to His private life, He seemed not to be a man of pleasure, nor of sorrow. He mingled with society to benefit it, and yet took no part at all in what was going on. 'I had heard many tell of what occurred when He was baptized, and from what His mother told me I was watching for a display of His divine power, if He had any, for I knew He could never be King of the Jews unless He did have help from on high. Once when we were attending a marriage-feast the wine gave out, and His mother told Him of it, and He said to the men to fill up some water-pots that were sitting near, and they put in nothing but water, for I watched them, but when they poured it out it was wine, for it was tasted by all at the feast, and when the master found it out he called for Jesus to honor Him, but He had disappeared. It seemed that He did not want to be popular, and this spirit displeased us, for we knew if He was to be the King of the Jews He must become popular with the Jews. His behavior angered His mother, for she was doing all she could to bring Him into notice, and to make Him popular among the people, and the people could not help liking Him when they saw Him. Another peculiarity was that in His presence everyone felt safe. There seemed to be an Almighty Power pervading the air wherever He went so that everyone felt secure, and believed that no harm could befall them if Jesus were present. As we were in our fishing-boats I saw Jesus coming out toward us, walking on the water. I knew that if He could make the waves support Him, He could me also. I asked Him if I might come to Him; He said to me to come, but when I saw the waves gathering around me I began to sink, and asked Him to help me. He lifted me up, and told me to have faith in God. On another occasion we were sailing on the sea, and there was a great storm. It blew at a fearful rate, and all on board thought they would be lost; we awaken the Master, and when He saw the raging of the storm He stretched out His hand and said, "Peace' be still!" and the wind ceased to blow, the thunder stopped, the lightnings withdrew, and the billowing sea seemed as quiet as a babe in its mother's arms – all done in one moment of time. This I saw with my own eyes, and from that time I was convinced that He was not a common man. Neither did He work by enchantment like the Egyptian thaumaturgists, for in all their tricks they never attack the laws of nature. In vain might they order the thunder to hush, or the winds to abate, or the lightnings to cease their flashing. Again, I saw this man while we were passing from Jericho. There was a blind man, who cried out to Him for mercy, and Jesus said to me, "Go, bring him near," and when I brought him near; Jesus asked him what he wanted. He said he wanted to see Him. Jesus said, "Receive thy sight," when he was not near enough for Jesus to lay His hands upon him or use any art. Thus were all His miracles performed. He did not act as the Egyptian necromancers. They use vessels, such as cups, bags, and jugs, and many other things to deceive. Jesus used nothing but His simple speech in such a way that all could understand Him, and it seemed as if the laws of nature were His main instruments of action, and that nature was as obedient to Him as a slave is to his master. I recall another occasion when a young man was dead, and Jesus loved his sisters. One of them went with Jesus to the tomb. He commanded it to be uncovered. The sister said, "Master, by this time he is offensive; he has been dead four days." Jesus said, "only have faith," and He called the young man by name, and he came forth out of the tomb, and is living to-day." And Peter proposed that I should see Him for myself.

Thus argued Peter and John. If Jesus had such power over nature and nature's laws, and power over death in others, He would have such power over death that He could lay down His life and take it up again, as He said He would do. As He proposed to bring hundreds of witnesses to prove all He says, and much more – witnesses whose veracity cannot be doubted – and as I had heard many of these things before from different men, both friends and foes (and although these things are related by His friends – that is, the friends of Jesus – yet these men talk like men of truth, and their testimony corroborates other evidence that I have from other sources, that convinces me that this is something that should not be rashly delt with, and seeing the humble trust and confidence of these men and women, besides, as John says, thousands of others equally strong in their belief, it throws me into great agitation. I feel some dreadful foreboding – a weight upon my heart. I cannot feel as a criminal from the fact that I was acting according to my best judgement with the evidence before me. I feel that I was acting in defense of God and my country, which I love better than my life, and if I was mistaken, I was honest in my mistake. And as we teach that the honesty of purpose gives character to the action, on this basis I shall try to clear myself of any charge, yet there is a conscious fear about my heart, so that I have no rest day or night. I feel sure that if I should meet Jesus I would fall dead at His feet; and it seemed to me that if I went out I should be sure to meet him.

In this state of conscious dread I remained investigating the scriptures to know more about the prophecies concerning this man, but found nothing to satisfy my mind. I locked my door and gave the guards orders to let no one in without first giving me notice. While thus engaged, with no one in the room but my wife and Annas, her father, when I lifted up my eyes, behold, Jesus of Nazareth stood before me. My breath stopped, my blood ran cold, and I was in the act of falling, when He spoke and said, 'Be not afraid, it is I. You condemned Me that you might go free. This is the work of My Father. Your only wrong is you have a wicked heart; this you must repent of. This last Lamb you have slain is the One that was appointed before the foundation; this Sacrifice is made for all men. Your other lambs were for those who offended them; this is for all, this is the last; it is for you if you will accept it. I died that you and all mankind might be saved.' At this He looked at me with such melting tenderness that it seemed to me I was nothing but tears, and my strength was all gone. I fell on my face at His feet as one that was dead. When Annas lifted me up Jesus was gone, and the door still locked. No one could tell when or where He went.

So, noble Masters, I do not feel that I can officiate as priest any more. If this strange personage is from God, and should prove to be the Savior we have looked for so long, and I have been the means of crucifying Him, I have no futher offerings to make for sin; but I will wait and see how these things will develop. And if He proves to be the Ruler that we are looking for, they will soon develop into something more grand in the future. His glory will increase; His influence will spread wider and wider, until the whole earth shall be full of His glory, and all the kingdoms of the world shall be His dominion. Such are the teachings of the prophets on this subject. Therefore you will appoint Jonathan, or someone, to fill the holy place.

[Note to the reader: soon after, Jonathan became high priest, even though history and the bible teach us differently. For when Caiaphas tore his vesture in anger during the trial where he accused Jesus of blasphemy, that transferred the high priesthood to Jesus. Now Jesus is the High Priest after the order of Melchisedec as stated in Hebrews chapter 4: 14, chapter 5: 4-6/9-10, chapter 6: 20, chapter 7: 1,12,17 & 21.]

Chapter 5

I PERSONALLY NEVER HEARD of this next person, whether in a history class, movie, documentary, or even just someone saying the name, that is, as far as I can remember, but I thought it interesting to understand a bit of his history and views.

VALLEUS PATERCULUS, B. 72, Found in the VATICAN at Rome.

Valleus Paterculus, was a Roman historian, was nineteen years old when Jesus was born. Most historians thought his work to be extinct. But two historians are known to have made reference to him, and they are Priscian and Tacitus, who spake of him as a descendant of an equestrian family from Campania. Valleus seemed to be a close friend of Caesar, who raised him by degrees until he became one of the great men of Rome, and for sixty years, commanded the Roman army. He returned to Rome in the year 31 and finished his work, which was called Historia Romania. He held the office of praetor when Augustus died, and while Vinceus was consul.

Valleus says that while in Judea he met a man called Jesus of Nazareth, who was one of the most remarkable characters he had ever seen; that he was more afraid of Jesus than of a whole army, for he cured all manner of disease and raised the dead, and when he cursed the orchards or fruit-trees for their barrenness, they instantly withered to their roots. After referring to the wonderful works of Jesus, he says that, although Jesus had such power, he did not use it to injure anyone, but seemed always inclined to help the poor. Valleus says the Jews were divided in their opinion of him, the poorer class claiming him as their King and deliverer from Roman authority, and that if Jesus should raise an army and give it the power he could sweep the world in a single day; but the rich Jews hated and cursed him behind his back, and called him an Egyptian necromancer, though they were as afraid of him as of death.

Next, is the report written by Pilate to the Emperor to explain what he understood and went through when he was faced with the case involving Jesus, and when he actually talked with him privately (before) the high priest brought him for sentencing.

The Report to TIBERIUS CAESAR from PONTIUS PILATE concerning the Events of JESUS

To Tiberius Caesar, Emperor of Rome.

"Noble Sovereign, Greeting:

The events of the last few days in my province have been of such a character that I will give the details in full as they occurred, as I should not be surprised if, in the course of time, they may change the destiny of our nation, for it seems of late that all the gods have ceased to be propitious. I am almost ready to say, cursed be the day that I succeeded Vallerius Flaceus in the government of Judea; for since then my life has been one of continual uneasiness and distress.

On my arrival at Jerusalem I took possession of the praetorium, and ordered a splendid feast to be prepared, to which I invited the tetrarch of Galilee, with the high priest and his officers. At the appointed hour no guests appeared. This I considered an insult offered to my dignity, and to the whole government which I represent. A few days after the high priest designed to pay me a visit. His deportment was grave and deceitful. He pretended that his religion forbade him and his attendants to sit at the table of the Romans, and eat and offer libations with them, but this was only a sanctimonious seeming, for his very countenance betrayed his hypocrisy. Although I thought it expedient to accept his excuse, from that moment I was convinced that the conquered had declared themselves the enemy of the conquerors; and I would warn the Romans to beware of the high priest of this country. They would betray their own mother to gain office and a luxurious living. It seems to me that, of conquered cities, Jerusalem is the most difficult to govern. So turbulent are the people that I lived in momentary dread of an insurrection. I have not soldiers sufficient to suppress it. I had only one centurion and a hundred men at my command. I requested a reinforcement from the prefect of Syria, who informed me that he had scarcely troops sufficient to defend his own province. An insatiate thirst for conquest to extend our empire beyond the means of defending it, I fear, will be the cause of the final overthrow of our whole government. I lived secluded from the masses, for I did not know what those priests might influence the rabble to do; yet I endeavored to ascertain, as far as I could, the mind and standing of the people.

Among the various rumors that came to my ears, there was one in particular that attracted my attention. A young man, it was said, had appeared in Galilee preaching with a noble unction a new law in the name of God that had sent him. At first I was apprehensive that his design was to stir up the people against the Romans, but my fears were soon dispelled. Jesus of Nazareth spoke rather as friend of the Romans than of the Jews. One day in passing by the place of Siloe, where there was a great concourse of people, I observed in the mist of the group a young man who was leaning against a tree, calmly addressing the multitude. I was told it was Jesus. This I could easily have suspected, so great was the difference between him and those listening to him. His golden-colored hair and beard gave to his appearance a celestial aspect. He appeared to be about thirty years of age. Never have I seen a sweeter or more serene countenance. What a contrast between him and his hearers, with their black beards and tawny complexions!

Unwilling to interrupt him with my presence, I continued my walk, but signified to my secretary to join the group and listen. My secretary's name is Manlius. He is the grandson of the chief of the conspirators who encamped in Etruria waiting for Cataline. Manlius had been for a long time an inhabitant of Judea, and is well acquainted with the Hebrew language. He was devoted to me, and worthy of my confidence. On entering the praetorium I found Manlius, who related to me the words Jesus had pronounced at Siloe. Never have I read in the works of the philosophers anything that can compare to the maxims of Jesus. One of the rebellious Jews, so numerous in Jerusalem, having asked Jesus if it was lawful to give tribute to Caesar, he replied; 'Render unto Caesar the things that belong to Caesar, and unto God the things that are God's.'

It was on account of the wisdom of his sayings that I granted so much liberty to the Nazarene; for it was in my power to have had him arrested, and exiled to Pontus; but that would have been contrary to the justice which has always characterized the Roman Government in all its dealings with men; this man was neither seditious nor rebellious; I extended to him my protection, unknown perhaps to himself. He was at liberty to act, to speak, to assemble and address the people, and to choose disciples, unrestrained by any praetorian mandate. Should it ever happen (may the gods avert the omen!), should it ever happen, I say, that the religion of our forefathers will be supplanted by the religion of Jesus, it will be to this noble toleration that Rome shall owe her premature death, while I, miserable wretch, will have been the instrument of what the Jews call Providence, and we call destiny.

This unlimited freedom granted to Jesus provoked the Jews – not the poor, but the rich and powerful. It is true, Jesus was severe on the latter, and this was a political reason, in my opinion, for not restraining the Nazarene. 'Scribes and Pharisees,' he would say to them, 'you are a race of vipers; you resemble painted sepulchres; you appear well unto men, but you have death within you.' At other times he would sneer at the alms of the rich and proud, telling them that the mite of the poor was more precious in the sight of God. Complaints were made at the praetorium against the insolence of Jesus.

I was even informed that some misfortune would befall him; that it would not be the first time that Jerusalem had stoned those who call themselves prophets; an appeal would be made to Caesar. However, my conduct was approved by the Senate, and I was promised a reinforcement after the termination of the Parthian war.

Being too weak to suppress an insurrection, I resolved upon adopting a measure that promised to restore the tranquillity of the city without subjecting the praetorium to humiliating concessions. I wrote to Jesus requesting an interview with him at the praetorium. He came. You know that in my veins flows the Spanish mixed with Roman blood – as incapable of fear as it is of weak emotion. When the Nazarene made his appearance, I was walking in my basilic, and my feet seemed fastened with an iron hand to the marble pavement, and I trembled in every limb as does a guilty culprit, though the Nazarene was as calm as innocence itself. When he came up to me he stooped, and by a signal sign he seemed to say to me, 'I am here,' though he spoke not a word. For some time I contemplated with admiration and awe this extraordinary type of man – a type of man unknown to our numerous painters, who have given form and figure to all the gods and the heroes. There was nothing about him that was repelling in its character, yet I felt too awed and tremulous to approach him.

'Jesus,' said I unto him at last – and my tongue faltered – 'Jesus of Nazareth, for the last three years I have granted you ample freedom of speech; nor do I regret it. Your words are those of a sage. I know not whether you have read Socrates or Plato, but this I know, there is in your discourse a majestic simplicity that elevates you far above those philosophers. The Emperor is informed of it, and I, his humble representative in this country, am glad of having allowed you that liberty of which you are so worthy. However, I must not conceal from you that your discourses have raised up against you powerful and inveterate enemies. Nor is this surprising. Socrates had his enemies, and he fell a victim to their hatred. Yours are doubly incensed – against you on account of your discourses being so severe upon their conduct; against me on account of the liberty I have afforded you. They even accuse me of being indirectly leagued with you for the purpose of depriving the Hebrews of the little civil power which Rome has left them. My request – I do not say my order – is, that you be more circumspect and moderate in your discourses in the future, and more considerate of them, lest you arouse the pride of your enemies, and they raise against you the stupid populace, and compel me to employ the instruments of law.'

The Nazarene calmly replied: 'Prince of the earth, your words proceed not from true wisdom. Say to the torrent to stop in the midst of the mountain-gorge; it will uproot the trees of the valley. The torrent will answer you that it obeys the laws of nature and the Creator. God alone knows whither flow the waters of the torrent. Verily I say unto you, before the rose of Sharon blossoms the blood of the just shall be split.'

'Your blood shall not be split,' said I, with deep emotion; 'you are more precious in my estimation on account of your wisdom than all the turbulent and proud Pharisees who abuse the freedom granted them by the Romans. They conspire against Caesar and convert his bounty into fear, impressing the unlearned that Caesar is a tyrant and seeks their ruin. Insolent wretches! They are not aware that the wolf of the Tiber sometimes clothes himself with the skin of the sheep to accomplish his wicked designs.

I will protect you against them. My praetorium shall be an asylum, sacred both day and night.'

Jesus carelessly shook his head, and said with a grave and divine smile; 'When the day shall have come there will be no asylums for the son of man, neither in the earth nor under the earth. The asylum of the just is there,' pointing to the heavens. 'That which is written in the books of the prophets must be accomplished.'

'Young man,' I answered, mildly, 'you will oblige me to convert my request into an order. The safety of the province which has been confided to my care requires it. You must observe more moderation in your discourses. Do not infringe my order. You know the consequences. May happiness attend you; farewell.'

'Prince of the earth,' replied Jesus, 'I come not to bring war into the world, but peace, love, and charity. I was born the same day on which Augustus Caesar gave peace to the roman world. Persecutions proceed not from me. I expect it from others, and will meet it in obedience to the will of my Father, who has shown me the way. Restrain, therefore, your worldly prudence. It is not in your power to arrest the victim at the foot of the tabernacle of expiation.'

So saying, he disappeared like a bright shadow behind the curtains of the basilic – to my great relief, for I felt a heavy burden on me, of which I could not relieve myself while in his presence.

To Herod, who then reigned in Galilee, the enemies of Jesus addressed themselves, to wreak their vengeance on the Nazarene. Had Herod consulted his own inclinations, he would have ordered Jesus immediately to be put to death; but, though proud of his royal dignity, yet he hesitated to commit an act that might lessen his influence with the Senate, or, like me, was afraid of Jesus. But it would never do for a Roman officer to be scared by a Jew. Previously to this, Herod called on me at the praetorium, and, on rising to take leave, after some trifling conversation, asked what was my opinion concerning the Nazarene. I replied that Jesus appeared to me to be one of those great philosophers that great nations sometimes produce; that his doctrines were by no means sacrilegious, and that the intentions of Rome were to leave him to that freedom of speech which was justified by his actions. Herod smiled maliciously, and, saluting me with ironical respect, departed.

The great feast of the Jews was approaching, and the intentions was to avail themselves of the popular exultation which always manifests itself at the solemnities of a passover. The city was overflowing with the tumultuous populace, clamoring for the death of the Nazarene. My emissaries informed me that the treasure of the temple had been employed in bribing the people. The danger was pressing. A Roman centurion had been insulted. I wrote to the Prefect of Syria for a hundred foot soldiers and as many cavalry. He declined. I saw myself alone with a handful of veterans in the mist of a rebellious city, too weak to suppress an uprising, and having no choice left but to tolerate it. They had seized upon Jesus, and the seditious rabble, although they had nothing to fear from the praetorium, believing, as their leaders had told them, that I winked at their sedition – continued vociferating; 'Crucify him! Crucify him!'

Three powerful parties had combined together at that time against Jesus: First, the Herodians and the Sadducees, whose seditious conduct seemed to have proceeded from double motives; they hated the Nazarene and were impatient of the Roman yoke. They never forgave me for entering the holy city with banners that bore the Roman Emperor; and although in this instance I had committed a fatal error, yet the sacrilege did not appear less heinous in their eyes. Another grievance also ranked in their bosoms. I had proposed to employ a part of the treasure of the temple in erecting edifices for public use. My proposal was scorned. The Pharisees were the avowed enemies of Jesus. They cared not for the government. They bore with bitterness the severe reprimands which the Nazarene for three years had been continually giving them wherever he went. Timid and too weak to act by themselves, they had embraced the quarrels of the Herodians and the Sadducees. Besides these three parties, I had to contend against the reckless and profligate populace, always ready to join a sedition, and to profit by the disorder and confusion that resulted therefrom.

Jesus was dragged before the High Priest and condemned to death. It was then that the High Priest, Caiaphas, performed a divisory act of submission. He sent his prisoner to me to confirm his condemnation and secure his execution. I answered him that, as Jesus was a Galilean, the affair came under Herod's jurisdiction, and ordered him to be sent thither. The wily tetrarch professed humility, and, protesting his deference to the lieutenant of Caesar, he committed the fate of the man to my hands. Soon my palace assumed the aspects of a besieged citadel. Every moment increased the number of the malcontents. Jerusalem was inundated with crowds from the mountains of Nazareth. All Judea appeared to be pouring into the city.

I had taken a wife from among the Gauls, who pretended to see into futurity. Weeping and throwing herself at my feet she said to me; 'Beware, beware, and touch not that man; for he is holy. Last night I saw him in a vision. He was walking on the waters; he was flying on the wings of the wind. He spoke to the tempest and to the fishes of the lake; all were obedient to him. Behold, the torrent in Mount Kedron flows with blood, the statues of Caesar are filled with gemonide; the columns of the interium have given away, and the sun is veiled in mourning like a vestal in a tomb. Ah! Pilate, evil awaits thee. If thou wilt not listen to the vows of thy wife, dread the curse of a Roman Senate; dread the frowns of Caesar.'

By this time the marble stairs groaned under the weight of the multitude. The Nazarene was brought back to me. I proceeded to the halls of justice, followed by my guards, and asked the people in a severe tone what they demanded.

'The death of the Nazarene,' was the reply.

'For what crime?'

'He has blasphemed; he has prophesied the ruin of the temple; he calls himself the Son of God, the Messiah, the King of the Jews.'

'Roman justice,' said I, 'punishes not such offences with death.'

'Crucify him! Crucify him!' cried the relentless rabble. The vociferations if the infuriated mob shook the palace to its foundations.

There was but one who appeared to be calm in the mist of the multitude; it was the Nazarene. After many fruitless attempts to protect him from the fury of his merciless persecutors, I adopted a measure which at the moment appeared to me to be the only one that could save his life. I proposed, as it was their custom to deliver a prisoner on such occasion, to release Jesus and let him go free, that he might be the scapegoat, as they called it; but they said that Jesus must be crucified. I then spoke to them of the inconsistency of their course as being incompatible with their laws, showing that no criminal judge could pass sentence on a criminal unless he had fasted one whole day; and that the sentence must have the consent of the Sanhedrim, and the signature of the president of that court; that no criminal could be executed on the same day his sentence was fixed, and the next day, on the day of his execution, the Sanhedrim was required to review the whole proceeding; also, according to their law, a man was stationed at the door of the court with a flag, and another a short way off on horseback to cry the name of the criminal and his crime, and the names of his witnesses, and to know if any one could testify in his favor; and the prisoner on his way to execution had the right to turn back three times, and to plead a new thing in his favor. I urged all these pleas, hoping they might awe them into subjection; but they still cried, 'Crucify him! Crucify him!'

I then ordered Jesus to be scourged, hoping this might satisfy them; but it only increased their fury. I then called for a basin, and washed my hands in the presence of the clamorous multitude, thus testifying that in my judgement Jesus of Nazareth had done nothing deserving of death; but in vain. It was his life they thirsted for.

Often in our civil commotions have I witnessed the furious anger of the multitude, but nothing could be compared to what I witnessed on this occasion. It might have been truly said that all the phantoms of the infernal regions had assembled at Jerusalem. The crowd appeared not to walk, but to be borne off and whirled as a vortex, rolling along in living waves from the portals of the praetorium even unto Mount Zion, with howling screams, shrieks, and vociferations such as were never heard in the seditions of the Pannonia, or in the tumults of the forum.

By degrees the day darkened like a winter's twilight, such as had been at the death of the great Julius Caesar. It was likewise the Ides of March. I, the continued governor of a rebellious province, was leaning against a column of my basilic, contemplating athwart the dreary gloom these fiends of Tartarus dragging to execution the innocent Nazarene. All around me was deserted. Jerusalem had vomited forth her indwellers through the funeral gate that leads to Gemonica. An air of desolation and sadness enveloped me. My guards had joined the cavalry, and the centurion, with a display of power, was endeavoring to keep order. I was left alone, and my breaking heart admonished me that what was passing at the moment appertained rather to the history of the gods than that of man. A loud clamor was heard proceeding from Golgotha, which, borne on the winds, seemed to announce an agony such as was never heard by mortal ears. Dark clouds lowered over the pinnacle of the temple, and setting over the city covered it as a veil. So dreadful were the signs that men saw in the heavens and on the earth that Dionysius the Areopagite is reported to have exclaimed, 'Either the author of nature is suffering or the universe is falling apart.'

Whilst these appalling scenes of nature were transpiring, there was a dreadful earthquake in lower Egypt, which filled everybody with fear, and scared the superstitious Jews almost to death. It is said Balthasar, an aged and learned Jew of Antioch, was found dead after the excitement was over. Whether he died from alarm or grief is not known. He was a strong friend of the Nazarene.

Near the first hour of night I threw my mantle around me, and went down into the city toward the gates of Golgotha. The sacrifice was consummated. The crowd was returning home, still agitated, it is true, but gloomy, taciturn, and desperate. What they had witnessed had stricken them with terror and remorse. I also saw my little Roman cohorts pass by mournfully, the standard-bearer having veiled his eagle in token of grief; and I overheard some of the Jewish soldiers murmuring strange words which I did not understand. Others were recounting miracles very like those which have so often smitten the Romans by the will of the gods. Sometimes groups of men and women would halt, then, looking back toward Mount Calvary, would remain motionless in expectation of witnessing some new prodigy.

I returned to the praetorium, sad and pensive. On ascending the stairs, the steps of which were still stained with the blood of the Nazarene, I perceived an old man in a suppliant posture, and behind him several Romans in tears. He threw himself at my feet and wept most bitterly. It is painful to see an old man weep, and my heart being already overcharged with grief, we, though strangers, wept together. And in truth it seemed that the tears lay very shallow that day with many whom I perceived in the vast concourse of people. I never witnessed such an extreme revulsion of feeling. Those who betrayed and sold him, those who testified against him, those who cried, 'Crucify him, we have his blood,' all slunk off like cowardly curs, and washed their teeth with vinegar. As I am told that Jesus taught a resurrection and a separation after death, if such should be the fact I am sure it commenced in this vast crowd.

'Father,' said I to him, after gaining control of my feelings, 'who are you, and what is your request?'

'I am Joseph of Arimathaea,' replied he, 'and am come to beg of you upon my knees the permission to bury Jesus of Nazareth.' (Note: Only relatives could make such a request, he is Jesus' uncle, Mary's mother's brother.)

'Your prayer is granted.' Said I to him; and at the same time I ordered Manlius to take some soldiers with him to superintend the interment, lest it should be profaned.

A few days after the sepulchre was found empty. His disciples proclaimed all over the country that Jesus had risen from the dead, as he had foretold. This created more excitement even than the crucifixion. As to its truth I cannot say for certain, but I have made some investigation of the matter; so you can examine for yourself, and see if I am in fault, as Herod represents.

Joseph buried Jesus in his own tomb. Whether he contemplated his resurrection or calculated to cut him another, I cannot tell. The day after he was buried one of the priest came to the praetorium and said they were apprehensive that his disciples intended to steal the body of Jesus and hide it, and then make it appear that he had risen from the dead, as he had foretold, and of which they were perfectly convinced. I sent him to the captain of the royal guard (Malcus) to tell him to take the Jewish soldiers, place as many around the sepulchre as were needed; then if anything should happen they could blame themselves, and not the Romans.

When the great excitement arose about the sepulchre being found empty, I felt a deeper solicitude than ever. I sent for Malcus, who told me he had placed his lieutenant, Ben Isham, with one hundred soldiers around the sepulchre. He told me that Isham and the soldiers were very much alarmed at what had occurred there that morning. I sent for this man Isham, who related to me, as near as I can recollect the following circumstances: He said that at about the beginning of the fourth watch they saw a soft and beautiful light over the sepulchre. He at first thought that the women had come to embalm the body of Jesus, as was their custom, but he could not see how they had gotten through the guards. While these thoughts were passing through his mind, behold, the whole place was lighted up, and there seemed to be crowds of the dead in their grave-clothes. All seemed to be shouting and filled with ecstasy, while all around and above was the most beautiful music he had ever heard; and the whole air seemed to be full of voices praising God. At this time there seemed to be a reeling and swimming of the earth, so that he turned so sick and faint that he could not stand on his feet. He said the earth seemed to swim from under him, and his senses left him, so that he knew not what did occur. I asked him what condition he was in when he came to himself. He said he was lying on the ground with his face down. I asked him if he could not have been mistaken as to the light. Was it not day that was coming in the East? He said at first he thought of that, but at a stone's cast it was exceedingly dark; and then he remembered it was too early for day. I asked him if his dizziness might not have come from being wakened up and getting up too suddenly, as it sometimes had that effect. He said he was not, and had not been sleep all night, as the penalty was death for him to sleep on duty. He said he had let some of the soldiers sleep at a time. Some were asleep then. I asked him how long the scene lasted. He said he didn't know, but the thought nearly an hour. He said it was hid by the light of day. I asked him if he had went to the sepulchre after he had come to himself. He said no, because he was afraid; that just as soon as relief came they all went to their quarters. I asked him if he had been questioned by the priest. He said he had. They wanted him to say it was an earthquake, and that they were asleep, and offered him money to say that the disciples came and stole Jesus; but he saw no disciples; he did not know that the body was gone until he was told. I asked him what was the private opinion of those priest he had conversed with. He said that some of them thought that Jesus was no man; that he was not a human being; that he was not the son of Mary; that he was not the same that was said to be born of a virgin in Bethlehem; that the same person had been on earth before with Abraham and Lot, and at many times and places.

It seemed to me that, if the Jewish theory be true, these conclusions are correct, for they are in accord with this man's life, as is known and testified by both friends and foes, for the elements were no more in his hands than in the hands of a potter. He could convert water into wine; he could change death into life, disease into health; he could calm the seas, still the storms, call up fish with a silver coin in its mouth. Now, I say, if he could do all these things, which he did, and many more, as the Jews all testify, and it was doing these things that created this enmity against him – he was not charged with criminal offenses, nor was he charged with violating any law, nor of wronging any individual in person, and all these facts are known to thousands, as well by his foes as by his friends – I am almost ready to say, as did Manulas at the cross, 'Truly this was the son of God.'

Now, noble Sovereign, this is as near the facts in the case as I can arrive at, and I have taken pains to make the statement very full, so that you may judge of my conduct upon the whole, as I hear that Antipater has said many hard things of me in this matter. With the promise of faithfulness and good wishes to my noble Sovereign,

I am your most obedient servant,

Pontius Pilate.

Chapter 6

AS IN THE HOLY Bible, the book of Job was not placed first in the cannon. But it is widely known that it is the oldest book in the Bible. So shall it be with this book. For, these are excerpts from the Book of Enoch, the first book ever written, by the man who actually invented writing. It is also known that he is the one who taught men to build cities. And, he is the first man that <u>never</u> died, (Genesis 5: 24). Also he was Noah's great grandfather, (Genesis 5: 29). It also explains some things that were left out in the book of Genesis, as in the events of chapter 6, and it gives us insight into the mindset of the angels that were involved.

Afterwards, I will show you some of the writings about the birth of and some of the things that Noah wrote. Some times, the insights on the things that people go through is quite interesting, even though those thoughts and actions might not make the headlines in any time.

But, there are too many chapters and verses to include them all in this book, so, anything left out will be because of tedium or non-relating items, which would not fit as well as those items that are to be included. Also there are too many "And" statements at the beginning of almost every sentence, therefore I removed many of them in order to allow the flow of the words to make more sense, but not to change the meaning or the concepts of the thinking involved. Thank you for your understanding.

Now, for your discernment...

The BOOK of ENOCH

From the Ethiopian Book of Enoch and
The Apocryphal writings.

Section 1.

Chapter 1

1. The words of the blessing of Enoch, wherewith he blessed the elect and righteous, who will be living in the day of tribulation, when all the wicked and godless are to be removed.

2. And he took up this parable and said – Enoch a righteous man, whose eyes were opened by God, saw the vision of the Holy One in the heavens, which the angels showed me, and from them I heard everything, and from them I understood as I saw, but not for this generation, but for a remote one which is to come.

3. Concerning the elect I said, and took up my parable concerning them: The Holy Great One will come forth from His dwelling,

4. The eternal God will tread upon the earth, …on Mount Sinai, and appear in the strength of His might from the heaven of heavens.

5. And all shall be smitten with fear and the watchers shall quake, and great fear and trembling shall seize them unto the ends of the earth.

6. The high mountains shall be shaken, and the high hills shall be made low, and shall melt like wax before the flame.

7. And the earth shall be wholly rent asunder, and all that is upon the earth shall perish, and there shall be a judgement upon all people.

8. But with the righteous He will make peace. And will protect the elect, and mercy shall be upon them. They shall all belong to God, they shall prosper, and they shall all be blessed. He will help them all, and light shall appear unto them, and He will make peace with them.

9. And behold! He cometh with ten thousands of His holy ones to execute judgement upon all and to destroy all the ungodly: and to convict all flesh of all the works of their ungodliness which they have ungodly committed. And of all the hard things ungodly sinners have spoken against Him.

Moving ahead to…

Chapter 6

1. It came to pass when the children of men had multiplied that in those days were born unto them beautiful and comely daughters.

2. The angels, the children of heaven, saw and lusted after them, and said to one another; 'Come, let us choose us wives from among the children of men and beget us children.'

3. Semjaza, who was their leader, said unto them: 'I fear ye will not indeed agree to do this deed, and I alone shall have to pay the penalty of a great sin.'

4. They all answered him and said: 'Let us all swear an oath, and all bind ourselves by mutual imprecations not to abandon this plan but to do this thing.'

5. Then sware they all together and bound themselves by mutual imprecations upon it.

6. And they were in all two hundred; who descended in the days of Jared on the summit of Mount Hermon, and they called it Mount Hermon, because they had sworn and bound themselves by mutual imprecations upon it.

7. These are the names of their leaders: Samlazaz, their leader, Aralba, Rameel, Kokabelel, Tamlel, Ramlel, Danel, Ezeqeel, Baraqijal, Asael, Armaros, Batarel, Ananel, Zaqlel, Samsapeel, Satarel, Tirel, Jomjael, and Sariel.

8. These are the chiefs of tens.

Chapter 7

1. And all the others together with them took unto themselves wives, and each chose for himself one, and they began to go in unto them and to defile themselves with them.

2. They taught them charms and enchantments, and the cutting of roots, and made them acquainted with plants.

3. They became pregnant, and they bare great giants, whose height was three thousand ells: who consumed all the acquisitions of men.

4. And when men could no longer sustain them, the giants turned against them and devoured mankind.

5. And they began to sin against birds, and beasts, and reptiles, and fish and to devour one another's flesh, and drink the blood.

6. Then the earth laid accusation against the lawless ones.

Chapter 8

1. Azazel taught men to make swords, and knives, and shields, and breastplates, and made known to them the metals of the earth and the art of working them, and bracelets, and ornaments, and the use of antimony, and the beautifying of the eyelids, and all kinds of costly stones, and all colouring tinctures.

2. And there arose much godlessness, and they committed fornications, and they were led astray, and became corrupt in all their ways.

3. Semjaza taught enchantments, and root-cuttings. Armaros the resolving of enchantments, Baraqijal astrology, Kokabel the constellations, Ezeqeel the knowledge of the clouds, Araqiel the signs of the earth, Shamsiel the sign of the sun, and Sariel the course of the moon.

4. And as men perished, they cried, and their cry went up to heaven.

Chapter 9

1. Then Michael, Uriel, Raphael, and Gabriel looked down from heaven and saw much blood being shed upon the earth, and all lawlessness being wrought upon the earth.

2. And they said one to another: 'The earth made without inhabitant cries the voice of their cryingst up to the gates of heaven.

3. And now to you, the holy ones of heaven, the souls of men make their suit, saying, "Bring our cause before the Most High."

4. They said to the Lord of the ages: "Lord of lords, God of gods, King of kings, and God of the ages, the throne of Thy glory remaineth unto all the generations of the ages, and Thy name holy and glorious an blessed unto all the ages!

5. Thou hast made all things, and power over all things hast Thou: and all things are naked and open in Thy sight, and Thou seest all things, and nothing can hide itself from Thee.

6. Thou seest what Azazel hath done, who hath taught all unrighteousness on earth and revealed the eternal secrets which were in heaven, which men were striving to learn: And Semjaza, to whom Thou hast given authority to bear rule over his associates.

7. And they have gone to the daughters of men upon the earth, and have slept with the women, and have defiled themselves, and revealed to them all kinds of sins.

8. And the women have borne giants, and the whole earth has thereby been filled with blood and unrighteousness.

9. Now, behold, the souls of those who have died are crying and making their suit to the gates of heaven, and their lamentations have ascended: and cannot cease because of the lawless deeds which are wrought on the earth.

10. knowest all things before they come to pass, Thou seest these things, Thou dost suffer them, and Thou dost not say to us what we are to do to them in regard to these.

Chapter 10

1. Then said the Most High, the Holy and Great One spake, and sent Uriel to the son of Lamech, and said to him:

2. 'Go to Noah and tell him in my name "Hide thyself!" and reveal to him the end that is approaching: that the whole earth will be destroyed, and a deluge is about to come upon the whole earth, and destroy all that is on it.

3. And now instruct him that he may escape and his seed may be preserved for all the generations of the world. And again the Lord said to Raphael: 'Bind Azazel hand and foot, and cast him into the darkness: and make an opening in the desert, which is in Dudael, and cast him therein.

4. Place upon him rough and jagged rocks, and cover him with darkness, and let him abide there forever, and cover his face that he may not see light.

5. And on the day of great judgement he shall be cast into the fire.

6. Heal the earth which the angels have corrupted, and proclaim the healing of the earth, that they may heal the plague, that all the children of men may not perish through all the secret things that the watchers have disclosed and have taught their sons.

7. The whole earth has been corrupted through the works that were taught by Azazel: to him ascribe all sin.

8. And to Gabriel said the Lord: 'Proceed against the bastards and the reprobates, and against the children of fornication: and destroy the children of the Watchers from amongst men: send them one against the other that they may destroy each other in battle: for length of days shall they not have.

9. No request that they make of thee shall be granted unto them fathers on their earth, for they hope to have an eternal life, and that each one of them will live five hundred years.'

10. And the Lord said unto Michael: 'Go, bind Semjaza and his associates who have united themselves with women so as to have defiled themselves with them in all their uncleanness.

11. When their sons have slain one another, and they have seen destruction of their beloved ones, bind them fast for seventy generations in the valleys of the earth, till the day of their judgement and of their consummation, till the judgement that is for ever and ever is consummated.

12. In those days they shall be led off to the abyss of fire; and to be tormented and the prison in which they shall be confined forever.

13. And whosoever shall be condemned and destroyed will from thenceforth be bound together with them to the end of all generations.

14. And destroy all the spirits of the reprobate and the children of the watchers, because they have wronged mankind.

15. Destroy all wrong from the face of the earth and let every evil work come to an end; and let the plant of righteousness and truth appear; and it shall prove a blessing; the works of righteousness and truth shall be planted in truth and joy for evermore.

16. And then shall all the righteous escape, and shall live till they beget thousands of children, and all the days of their youth and their old age shall come in peace.

17. And then shall the whole earth be tilled in righteousness, and shall all be planted with trees and be full of blessing.

18. And all desirable trees shall be planted on it, and they shall plant vines on it; and the vine which they plant thereon shall yield wine in abundance, and as for all the seed which is sown thereon each measure shall bear a thousand, and each measure of olives shall yield ten presses of oil.

19. Cleanse thou the earth from all oppression, and from all unrighteousness, and from all sin, and from all godlessness; and all the uncleanness that is wrought upon the earth destroy from off the earth.

20. All the children of men shall become righteous, and all nations shall offer adoration and shall praise Me, and all shall worship Me.

21. The earth shall be cleansed from all defilement, and from all sin, and from all punishment, and from all torment, and I will never again send upon it from generation to generation and forever.

Chapter 11

1. And in those days I will open the store chambers of blessing which are in the heaven, so as to send them down upon the earth over the work and labour of the children of men.

2. Truth and peace shall be associated together throughout all the days of the world and throughout all the generations of men.

Chapter 12

1. Before these things Enoch was hidden, and no one of the children of men knew where he was hidden, and where he abode, and what had become of him.

2. And his activities had to do with the Watchers, and his days were with the holy ones.

3. I Enoch was blessing the Lord of majesty and the King of the ages, and lo! The Watchers called me-Enoch the scribe and said to me:

4. 'Enoch, thou scribe of righteousness, go declare to the Watchers of the heaven who have left the high heaven, the holy eternal place, and have defiled themselves with women, and have done as the children of earth do, and have taken unto themselves wives.

5. You have wrought great destruction on the earth. And ye shall have no peace nor forgiveness of sin; and inasmuch as they delighted themselves in their children, the murder of their beloved ones shall they lament, and shall make supplications unto eternity, but mercy and peace shall ye not attain.'

Chapter 13

1. And Enoch went and said: 'Azazel, thou shalt have no peace; a sever sentence has gone forth against thee to put thee in bonds; and thou shalt not have toleration nor request granted to thee, because of the unrighteousness which thou hast taught, and because of all the works of godlessness and sin which thou hast shown to men.'

2. Then I went and spake to them all together, and they were all afraid, and fear and trembling seized them.

3. They besought me to draw up a petition for them that they might find forgiveness, and to read their petition in the presence of the Lord of heaven.

4. For from thenceforward they could not speak to God nor lift up their eyes to heaven for shame of their sins for which they had been condemned.

5. Then I wrote out their petition, and the prayer in regard to their spirits and their deeds individually and in regard to their request that they should have forgiveness and length.

6. And I went off and sat down at the waters of Dan, in the land of Dan, to the south of the west of Hermon: I read their petition till I fell asleep.

7. And behold a dream came to me, and visions fell down upon me, and I saw visions of chastisements, and a voice came bidding I to tell it to the sons of heaven, and reprimand them.

8. When I awaked, I came unto them, and they were all sitting gathered together, weeping in Abelsjail, which is between Lebanon and Seneser, with their faces covered.

9. And I recounted before them all the visions which I had seen in sleep, and I began to speak the words of righteousness, and to reprimand the heavenly Watchers.

Chapter 14

1. The book of the words of righteousness, and of the reprimand of the eternal Watchers in accordance with the command of the Holy Great One in that vision.

2. I saw in my sleep what I will now say with a tongue of flesh and with the breath of my mouth: which the Great One has given to men to converse therewith and understand with the heart.

3. As He has created and given to man the power of understanding the word of wisdom, so hath He created me also and given me the power of reprimanding the Watchers, the children of heaven.

4. I wrote out your petition, and in my vision it appeared thus, that your petition will not be granted unto you throughout all the days of eternity, and that judgement has been finally passed upon you: yea your petition will not be granted unto you.

5. And from henceforth you shall not ascend into heaven unto all eternity, and in bounds of the earth the decree has gone forth to bind you for all the days of the world.

6. And previously you shall have no pleasure in them, but they shall fall before you by the sword.

7. Your petition on their behalf shall not be granted, nor yet on your own: even though you weep and pray and speak all the words contain in the writing which I have written.

8.   And the vision clouds invited me and a mist summoned me and the course of the stars and the lightnings sped and hastened me, and wings in the vision caused me to fly and lifted me upward, and bore me into heaven.

9.   I went in till I drew nigh to a wall which is built of crystals and surrounded by tongues of fire: and it began to affright me.

10. And I went into the tongues of fire and drew nigh to a large house which was built of crystals: and the walls of the house were like a tessellated floor of crystals, and its groundwork was of crystal.

11. Its ceiling was like the path of the stars and the lightnings, and between them were fiery cherubim, an their heaven was as clear as water.

12. A flaming fire surrounded the walls, and its portals blazed with fire.

13. And I entered into that house, and it was hot as fire and cold as ice: there were no delights of life therein: fear covered me, and trembling got hold upon me.

14. As I quaked and trembled, I fell upon my face. And I beheld a vision. And lo! There was a second house, greater than the former, and the entire portal stood open before me, and it was built of flames of fire.

15. In every respect it so excelled in splendor and magnificence and extent that I cannot describe to you its splendor and its extent.

16. Its floor was of fire, above it were lightnings and the path of the stars, and its ceiling also was a flaming fire.

17. I looked and saw therein a lofty throne: its appearance was as crystal, the wheels thereof as the shining sun, and there was the vision of cherubim.

18. From underneath the throne came streams of flaming fire so that I could not look thereon.

19. The Great Glory sat thereon, and His raiment shone mere brightly than the sun and was whiter than any snow.

20. None of the angels could enter and could behold His face by reason of the magnificence and glory and no flesh could behold Him.

21. The flaming fire was round about Him, and a great fire stood before Him, and none could draw nigh Him: ten thousand times ten thousand were before Him, yet He needed no counselor.

22. And the most holy ones who were nigh to Him did not leave by night nor depart from Him.

23. Until then I had been prostrate on my face, trembling: and the Lord called me with His own mouth, and said to me: 'Come hither, Enoch, and hear my word.' And one of the holy ones came to me and waked me, and He made me rise up and approach the door: and I bowed my face downwards.

Chapter 15

1.   He answered and said to me, and I heard His voice: 'Fear not, Enoch, thou righteous man and scribe of righteousness: approach hither and hear my voice.

2. And go, say to the Watchers of heaven, who have sent thee to intercede for them: "You should intercede for men, and not men for you: whereof have ye left the high, holy, and eternal heaven, and lain with women, and defiled yourselves with the daughters of men and taken to yourselves with the daughters of men and taken to yourselves wives, and done like the children of earth, and begotten giants for sons?

3. Though ye were holy, spiritual, living the eternal life, you have defiled yourselves with the blood of women, and have begotten with the blood of the flesh, and, as the children of men, have lusted after flesh and blood as those also do who die and perish.

4. Therefore have I given them wives also that they might impregnate them, and beget children by them, that thus nothing might be wanting to them on earth.

5. But you were formerly spiritual, living the eternal life, and immortal for all generations of the world.

6. And therefore I have not appointed wives for you, for as for the spiritual ones of the heaven, in heaven is their dwelling.

7. And now, the giants, who are produced from the spirits and flesh, shall be called evil spirits upon the earth, and on the earth be their dwelling.

8. Evil spirits have proceeded from their bodies; because they are born from men and from holy Watchers is their beginning and primal origin; they shall be evil spirits on the earth, and evil spirits shall they be called.

9. The spirits of the giants afflict, oppress, destroy, attack, do battle, and work destruction on the earth, and cause trouble: they take no food, but nevertheless hunger and thirst, and cause offences.

10. And these spirits shall rise up against the children of men and against the women, because they have proceeded from them.

Chapter 16

1. From the days of the slaughter and destruction and death of the giants, from the souls of whose flesh the spirits, having gone forth, shall destroy without incurring judgement – thus shall they destroy until the day of consummation, the great judgement in which the age shall be consummated, over the Watchers and the godless, yea, shall be wholly consummated.

2. And now as to the Watchers who have sent thee to intercede for them, who had been aforetime in heaven, say unto them: You have been in heaven, but all the mysteries had not yet been revealed to you, and you knew the worthless ones, and these in the hardness of your hearts you have made known to the women, and through these mysteries women and man work much evil on earth."

3. Say to them therefore: "You shall have no peace."

Chapter 17

1. They took me to a place in which those who were like flaming fire, and, when they wished, they appeared as men.

2. And they brought me to the place of darkness, and to a mountain the point of whose summit reached to heaven.

3. And I saw the places of the luminaries and the treasuries of the stars and of the thunder and in the uttermost depths, where were a fiery bow and arrows and their quiver, and a fiery sword and all the lightnings.

4. And they took me to the living waters, and to the fire of the west, which receives every setting of the sun.

5. I came to a river of fire in which the fire flows like water and discharges itself into the great sea towards the west.

6. I saw the great rivers and came to the great river and to the great darkness, and went to the place where no flesh walks.

7. I saw the mountains of the darkness of winter and the place whence all the waters of the deep flow.

8. I saw the mouths of all the rivers of the earth and the mouth of the deep.

Chapter 18

1. I saw the treasuries of all the winds: I saw how He had furnished with them the whole creation and the firm foundations of the earth.

2. And I saw the corner stone of the earth: I saw the four winds which bear the firmament of the heaven.

3. And I saw how the winds stretch out the vaults of heaven, and have their station between heaven and earth: these are the pillars of the heaven.

4. I saw the winds of heaven, which turn and bring the circumference of the sun and all the stars to their setting.

5. I saw the winds on the earth carrying the clouds. I saw the paths of the angels. I saw at the end of the earth the firmament of the heaven above.

6. And I proceeded and saw a place which burns day and night, where there are seven mountains of magnificent stones, three towards the east, and three towards the south.

7. As for those towards the east, was of coloured stone, and one of pearl, and one of jacinth, and those towards the south of red stone.

8. But the middle one reached to heaven like the throne of God, of alabaster, and the summit of the throne was of sapphire.

9. And I saw a flaming fire. Beyond these mountains is a region at the end of the great earth: there the heavens were completed.

10. And I saw a deep abyss, with columns of heavenly fire, and among them I saw columns of fire fall, which were beyond measure alike towards the height and towards the depth.
11. Beyond that abyss I saw a place which had no firmament of the heaven above, and no firmly founded earth beneath it: there was no water upon it, and no birds, but it was a waste and horrible place.
12. I saw there seven stars like great burning mountains, and to me, when I inquired regarding them, the angel said: 'This place is the end of heaven and earth: this has become a prison for the stars and the host of heaven.
13. The stars which roll over the fire are they which have transgressed the commandment of the Lord in the beginning of their rising, because they did not come forth at their appointed times.
14. And He was wroth with them, and bound them till the time when their guilt should be consummated for ten thousand years.

Chapter 19

1. And Uriel said to me: 'Here shall stand the angels who have connected themselves with women, and their spirits assuming many different forms are defiling mankind and shall lead them astray into sacrificing to demons as gods, till the day of the great judgement in which they shall be judged till they are made an end of.
2. The women also of the angels who went astray shall become sirens.' And I Enoch, alone saw the vision, the ends of all things: and no man shall see as I have seen.

Chapter 20

1. These are the names of the holy angels who watch. Uriel, one of the holy angels, who is over the world and over Tartarus.
2. Raphael, one of the holy angels, who is over the spirits of men. Raguel, one of the holy angels who takes vengeance on the world of the luminaries.
3. Michael, one of the holy angels, to wit, he that is set over the best part of mankind and over chaos. Saraqael, one of the holy angels, who is set over the spirits, who sin in the spirit.
4. Gabriel, one of the holy angels, who is over Paradise and the serpents and Cherubim. Remiel, one of the holy angels, whom God set over those who rise.

Chapter 21

1. And I proceeded to where things were chaotic. And I saw there something horrible: I saw neither a heaven above nor a firmly founded earth, but a place chaotic and horrible.
2. And there I saw seven stars of the heaven bound together in it, like great mountains and burning with fire.

3. Then I said: 'For what sin are they bound, and on what account have they been cast in hither?' Then said Uriel, one of the holly angels, who was with me, and was chief over them, and said: 'Enoch, why dost thou ask and why art thou eager for the truth?

4. These are of the number of the stars of heaven, which have transgressed the commandments of the Lord, and are bound here till ten thousand years, the time entailed by their sins, are consummated.

5. From thence I went to another place, which was still more horrible than the former, and I saw a horrible thing: a great fire there which burnt and blazed, and the place was cleft as far the abyss, being full of great descending columns of fire: neither its extent or magnitude could I see, nor could I conjecture.

6. Then I said: 'How fearful is the place and how terrible to look upon! Then Uriel answered me, one of the holy angels who was with me, and said unto me: 'Enoch, why hast thou such fear and affright?'

7. And I answered: 'Because of this fearful place, and because of the spectacle of the pain.' And he said unto me: 'This place is the prison of the angels, and here they will be imprisoned for ever.'

Because of the tedious nature of the next chapters I will move on to:

Chapter 24

1. From thence I went to another place of the earth, and he showed me a mountain range of fire which burned day and night.

2. And I went beyond it and saw seven magnificent mountains all different each from the other, and the stones were magnificent and beautiful, magnificent as a whole, of glorious appearance and fair exterior: three towards the east, one founded on the other, and three towards the south, one upon the other, and deep rough ravines, no one of which joined with any other.

3. The seventh mountain was in the mist of these, and it excelled them in height, resembling the seat of a throne: and fragrant trees encircled the throne.

4. Among them was a tree such as I had never yet smelt, neither was any amongst them nor were others like it: it had a fragrance beyond all fragrance, and its leaves and blooms and wood wither not for ever: and its fruit is beautiful, and its fruit resembles the dates of a palm.

5. Then I said: 'How beautiful is the tree, and fragrant, and its leaves are fair, and its blooms very delightful in appearance.'

6. Then answered Michael, one of the holy and honored angels who was with me, and was their leader.

Chapter 25

1. And he said unto me: 'Enoch, why dost thou ask me regarding the fragrance of the tree, and why dost thou wish to learn the truth?' Then I answered him saying: 'I wish to know everything, but especially about this tree.'

2. And he answered saying: 'This high mountain which thou hast seen, whose summit is like the throne of God, is His throne, where the Holy Great One, the Lord of Glory, the Eternal King, will sit, when He shall come down to visit the earth with goodness.

3. As for this judgement, when He shall take vengeance on all and bring all things to its consummation forever.

4. It shall then be given to the righteous and holy. Its fruit shall be for food to the elect: it shall be transplanted to the holy place, to the temple of the Lord, the Eternal King.

5. Then shall they rejoice with joy and be glad, and its fragrance shall be in their bones, and they shall live a long life on earth, such as thy fathers lived: and in their days shall no sorrow or plague or torment or calamity touch them.

6. Then blessed I the God of Glory, the Eternal King, who hath prepared such things for the righteous, and hath created them and promised to give to them.

Chapter 32

1. And after these fragrant odors, as I looked towards the north over the mountains I saw seven mountains full of choice nard and fragrant trees and cinnamon and pepper.

2. And thence I went over the summits of all these mountains, far towards the east of the earth and passed above the …(unintelligible script)…I came to the Garden of Righteousness, I and from afar off trees more numerous than I, these trees and great-two trees there, very great, beautiful, and glorious, and magnificent, and the tree of knowledge, whose holy fruit they eat and know great wisdom.

3. That tree in height is like the fir, and its leaves are like the Carob tree: and its fruit is like the clusters of a vine, very beautiful: and the fragrance of the tree penetrates afar.

4. Then I said: 'How beautiful is the tree, and how attractive is its look!' Then Raphael the holy angel, who was with me, answered me and said: 'This is the tree of wisdom, of which thy father old in years and aged mother, who were before thee, have eaten, and they learnt wisdom and their eyes were opened, and they knew that they were naked and they were driven out of the garden.'

Chapter 42

1. Wisdom found no place where she might dwell; then a dwelling-place was assigned her in the heavens.

2. Wisdom went forth to make her dwelling among the children of men. And found no dwelling place. Wisdom returned to her place, and took her seat among the angels.

3. And unrighteousness went forth from her chambers: whom she sought not she found, and dwelt with them, as rain in a desert, and dew on a thirsty land.

Chapter 45

1. This is the second Parable concerning those who deny the name of the dwelling of the holy ones and the Lord of Spirits.

2. Into the heaven they shall not ascend, and on the earth they shall not come: such shall be the lot of the sinners who have denied the name of the Lord of Spirits, who are thus preserved for the day of suffering and tribulation.

3. On that day Mine Elect One shall sit on the throne of glory and shall try their works, and their places of rest shall be innumerable. And their souls shall grow strong within them when they see Mine Elect Ones, and those who have called upon My glorious name.

4. Then will I cause Mine Elect One to dwell among them. And I will transform the heaven and make it an eternal blessing and light.

5. And I will transform the earth and make it a blessing: and I will cause Mine elect ones to dwell upon it: but the sinners and evil-doers shall not set foot thereon.

6. For I have provided and satisfied with peace My righteous ones and have caused them to dwell before Me: but for the sinners there is judgment impending with Me, so that I shall destroy them from the face of the earth.

Chapter 46

1. And there I saw One who had a head of days, and His head was white like wool, and with Him was another being whose countenance had the appearance of a man, and his face was full of graciousness like one of the holy angels.

2. And I asked the angel who went with me and showed me all the hidden things, concerning that Son of Man, who he was, and whence he was, why he went with the Head of Days?

3. And he answered and said unto me: 'This is the son of righteousness, with whom dwelleth righteousness, and who revealeth all the treasures of that which is hidden, because the Lord of Spirits hath chosen him, and whose lot hath the pre-eminence before the Lord of Spirits in uprightness for ever.

4. This Son of Man, whom thou hast seen shall raise up the kings and the mighty from their seats, shall loosen the reins of the strong, and break the teeth of the sinners.

5. Because they do not extol and praise Him, nor humbly acknowledge whence the kingdom was bestowed upon them.

6. He shall put down the countenance of the strong, and shall fill them with shame. And darkness shall be their dwelling and worms shall be their bed, and they shall have no hope of rising from their beds, because they do not extol the name of the Lord of Spirits.

7. These are they who judge the stars of heaven, and tread upon the earth and dwell upon it.

8. And all their deeds manifest unrighteousness, their power rests upon their riches, and their faiths is in the gods which they have made with their hands, and they deny the name of the Lord of Spirits, and they persecute the houses of His congregations, and the faithful who hang upon the name of the Lord of Spirits.

Chapter 60

A Fragment of the Book of Noah

1. In the year 500, in the seventh month, on the fourteenth day of the month in the life of Enoch. In that Parable I saw how a mighty quaking made the heaven of heavens to quake, and the host of the Most High, and the angels, a thousand thousands and ten thousand times ten thousand, were disquieted with a great disquiet.

2. The Head of Days sat on the throne of His glory, and the angels and the righteous stood around Him.

3. And a great trembling seized me, and fear took hold of me, and my loins gave way, and dissolved were my reins, and I fell upon my face.

4. Michael sent another angel from among the holy ones and he raised me up, and when he had raised me up my spirit returned; for I had not been able to endure the look of this host, and the commotion and the quaking of the heaven.

5. And Michael said unto me: 'Why art thou disquieted with such a vision? Until this day lasted the day of His mercy; and He hath been merciful and long-suffering towards those who dwell on the earth.

6. When the day, the power, the punishment, and the judgment come, which the Lord of Spirits hath prepared for those who worship not the righteous law, for those who deny the righteous judgment, and for those who take His name in vain-that day is prepared, for the elect a covenant, but for sinners inquisition.

7. When the punishment of the Lord of Spirits shall rest upon them, it shall rest in order that the punishment of the Lord of Spirits may not come, in vain, and it shall slay the children with their mothers and the children with their fathers.

8. Afterwards the judgment shall take place according to His mercy and His patience.'

9. On that day were two monsters parted, a female monster named Leviathan, to dwell in the abysses of the ocean over the fountains of the waters.

10.   But the male is named Behemoth, who occupied with his breast a waste wilderness named Duidian, on the east of the garden where the elect and righteous dwell, where my grandfather was taken up, the seventh from Adam, the first man whom the Lord of Spirits created.

11.   I besought the other angel that he should show me the might of those monsters, how they were parted one day and cast, the one into the abysses of the sea, and the other onto the dry land of the wilderness.

12.   And he said to me: 'Thou son of man, herein thou dost seek to know what is hidden.'

13.   And the other angel who went with me and showed me what was hidden told me what is first and last in the heaven in the height, and beneath the earth in the depth, and at the ends of the heaven, and on the foundation of the heaven.

14.   And the chambers of the winds, and how the winds are divided, and how they are weighed, and the portals of the winds are reckoned, each according to the power of the wind, and the power of the lights of the moon, and according to the power that is fitting: and the divisions of the stars according to their names, and how all the divisions are divided.

15.   And the thunders according to the places where they fall, and all the divisions that are made among the lightnings that it may lighten, and their host that they may at once obey.

16.   For the thunder has places of rest which are assigned to it while it is waiting for its peal; and the thunder and lightning are inseparable, and although not one and undivided, they both go together through the spirit and separated not.

17.   For when the lightning lightens, the thunder utters its voice, and the spirit enforces a pause during the peal, and divides equally between them; for the treasury of their peals in like the sand, and each one of them as it peals is held in with a bridle, and turned back by the power of the spirit, and pushes forward according to the many quarters of the earth.

18.   The spirit of the sea is masculine and strong, and according to the might of his strength he draws it back with rein, and in like manner it is driven forward and disperses amid all the mountains of the earth.

19.   The spirit of the hoarfrost is his own angel, and the spirit of the hail is a good angel.

20.   And the spirit of the snow has forsaken his chambers on account of his strength – there is a special spirit therein, and that which ascends from it is like smoke, and its name is frost.

21.   The spirit of the mist is not united with them in their chambers, but it has a special chamber; for its course is glorious both in light and in darkness, and in winter and in summer, and in its chambers is an angel.

22. The spirit of the dew has its dwelling at the ends of heaven, and is connected with the chambers of the rain, and its course is in winter and summer: and its clouds and the clouds of the mist are connected, and the one gives to the other.

23. When the spirit of the rain goes forth from its chamber, the angels come and open the chamber and lead it out, and when it is diffused over the whole earth it unites with the water on the earth.

24. And whensoever it unites with the water on the earth…for the waters are for those who dwell on the earth; for they are nourishment for the earth from the Most High who is in heaven: therefore there is a measure for the rain, and the angels take it in charge.

25. These things I saw towards the Garden of the Righteous.

26. And the angel of peace who was with me said to me: 'These two monsters, prepared conformably to the greatness of God, shall feed.

Chapter 61

1. I saw in those days how long cords were given to those angels, and they took to themselves wings and flew, and they went towards the north.

2. I asked the angel, saying unto him: 'Why have those taken these cords and gone off?' And he said unto me: 'They have gone to measure.'

3. The angel who went with me said unto me: 'These shall bring the measures of the righteous, and the ropes of the righteous to the righteous, that they may stay themselves on the name of the Lord of Spirits for ever and ever.

4. The elect shall dwell with the elect, and those are the measures which shall be given to faith and which shall strengthen righteousness.

5. And those measures shall reveal all the secrets of the depths of the earth, and those who have been destroyed by the desert, and those who have been destroyed by the beasts, and those who have been destroyed by the fish of the sea, that they may return and stay themselves on the day of the Elect One.

6. For none shall be destroyed before the Lord of Spirits, and none can be destroyed.

7. And all whom dwell above in the heaven received a command and power and one voice and one light like unto fire.

8. And that One, their first words they blessed, and extolled and lauded with wisdom, and they were wise in utterance and in the spirit of life.

9. And the Lord of Spirits placed the Elect One on the throne of glory.

10. He shall judge all the works of the holy above in the heaven, and in the balance shall their deeds be weighed.

11. When he shall lift up his countenance to judge their secret ways according to the word of the name of the Lord of Spirits, and their path according to the way of the righteous judgment of the Lord of Spirits.

12. Then shall they all with one voice speak and bless, and glorify and extol and sanctify the name of the Lord of Spirit.

13. He will summon all the host of the heavens, and all the holy ones above, and the host of God, the Cherubic, Seraphim and Ophannin, and all the angels of power, and all the angels of principalities, and the Elect One, and the other powers on the earth and over the water on that day shall raise one voice, and bless and glorify and exalt in the spirit of faith, and in the spirit of wisdom, and in the spirit of patience, and in the spirit of mercy, and in the spirit of judgement and of peace, and in the spirit of goodness, and shall all say with one voice: "Blessed is He, and may the name of the Lord of Spirits be blessed for ever and ever."

14. All who sleep not above in heaven shall bless Him: all the holy ones who are in heaven shall bless Him.

15. And all the elect who dwell in the garden of life: and every of light who is able to bless, and glorify, and extol, and hallow Thy blessed name, and all flesh shall beyond measure glorify and bless Thy name for ever and ever.

16. For great is the mercy of the Lord of Spirits, He is long-suffering, and all His works and all that He has created He has revealed to the righteous and elect in the name of the Lord of Spirits.

Chapter 62

1. Thus the Lord commanded the kings and the mighty and the exalted, and those who dwell on the earth, and said: 'Open your eyes and lift up your horns if ye are able to recognize the Elect One.'

2. The Lord of Spirits seated Him on the throne of His glory, and the spirit of righteousness was poured out upon him, and the word of his mouth slays all the sinners. All the unrighteous are destroyed from before His face.

3. And there shall stand up in that day all the kings and the mighty, and the exalted and those who hold the earth, and they shall see and recognize how He sits on the throne of his glory, and righteousness is judged before him, and no lying word is spoken before him.

4. Then shall pain come upon them as on a woman in travail, when her child enters the mouth of the womb, and she has pain in bringing forth.

5. One portion of them shall look on the other, and they shall be terrified, and they shall be downcast of countenance, and pain shall seize them, when they see that Son of Man sitting on the throne of His glory.

6. The kings and the mighty and all who possess the earth shall bless and glorify and extol Him who rules over all, who was hidden.

7. For from the beginning the Son of Man was hidden, and the Most High preserved Him in the presence of His might, and revealed Him to the elect.

8. And the congregation of the elect and the holy shall be sown, and all the elect shall stand before Him on that day.

9. All the kings and the mighty and the exalted and those who rule the earth shall fall down before Him on their faces, and worship and set their hope upon that Son of Man, and petition him and supplicate for mercy at His hands.

10. Nevertheless that Lord of Spirits will so press them that they shall hastily go forth from His presence, and their faces shall be filled with shame, and the darkness grow deeper on their faces.

11. He will deliver them to the angels for punishment, to execute vengeance on them because they have oppressed His children and His elect.

12. They shall be a spectacle for the righteous and for His elect: they shall rejoice over them, because the wrath of the Lord of Spirits resteth upon them, and His sword is drunk with their blood.

13. And the righteous and elect shall be saved on that day, and they shall never thenceforward see the face of the sinners and unrighteous.

14. The Lord of Spirits will abide over them, and with that Son of Man shall they eat and lie down and rise up forever and ever.

15. The righteous and elect shall have risen from the earth, and ceased to be of downcast countenance.

16. And they shall have been clothed with garments of glory, and these shall be the garments of life from the Lord of Spirits: and your garments shall not grow old, nor your glory pass away before the Lord of Spirits.

Chapter 63

1. In those days shall the mighty and the kings who possess the earth implore to grant them a little respite from His angels of punishment to whom they were delivered, that they might fall down and worship before the Lord of Spirits, and confess their sins before Him.

2. They shall bless and glorify the Lord of Spirits, and say: Blessed is the Lord of Spirits and the Lord of Kings, and the Lord of the mighty and the Lord of the rich, and the Lord of glory and the Lord of wisdom.

3. And splendid in every secret thing is Thy power from generation to generation, and Thy glory for ever and ever: deep are all Thy secrets and innumerable, and Thy righteousness is beyond reckoning.

4. We have now learnt that we should glorify and bless the Lord of Kings and Him who is King ever all kings.'

5. And they shall say: 'Would that we had rest to glorify and give thanks and confess our faith before His glory! And now we long for a little rest but find it not, we follow hard upon and obtain not, and light has vanished from before us, and darkness is our dwelling-place for ever and ever.

6. For we have not believed before Him, nor glorified the name of the Lord of Spirits, but our hope was in the scepter of our kingdom, and in our glory.

7. In the day of our suffering and tribulation He saves us not, and we find no respite for confession that our Lord is true in all His works, and in His judgements and His justice, and His judgments have no respect of persons.

8. And we pass away from before His face on account of our works, and all our sins are reckoned up in righteousness.'

9. Now they shall say unto themselves: 'Our souls are full of unrighteous gain, but it does not prevent us from descending from the mist thereof into the burden of Sheol.'

10. After that their faces shall be filled with darkness and shame before that Son of Man.

11. And they shall be driven from His presence, and the sword shall abide before His face in their mist.

12. Thus spake the Lord of Spirits: 'This is the ordinance and judgement with respect to the mighty and the kings and the exalted and those who possess the earth before the Lord of Spirits.'

Chapter 64

1. And other forms I saw hidden in that place.

2. I heard the voice of the angel saying: 'These are the angels who descended to the earth, and revealed what was hidden to the children of men and seduced the children of men into committing sin.'

Chapter 65

1. In those days Noah saw the earth that it had sunk down and its destruction was nigh. And he arose from thence and went to the ends of the earth, and cried aloud to his grandfather Enoch, and Noah said three times with an emoted voice: 'Hear me, hear me, hear me! And I said unto him: 'Tell me what it is that is falling out on the earth that the earth is in such evil plight and shaken, lest perchance I shall perish with it?'

2. And thereupon there was a great commotion on the earth, and a voice was heard from heaven, and I fell on my face.

3. And Enoch my grandfather came and stood by me, and said unto me: 'Why hast thou cried unto me with a bitter cry and weeping?

4. A command has gone forth from the presence of the Lord concerning those who dwell on the earth that their ruin is accomplished because they have learnt all the secrets of the angels, and all the violence of the Satans, and all their powers – the most secret ones – and all the power of those who practice sorcery, and the power of witchcraft, and the power of those who make molten images for the whole earth.

5. And how silver is produced from the dust of the earth, and how soft metal originates in the earth.

6. For lead and tin are not produced from the earth like the first: it is a fountain that produces them, and an angel stands therein, and that angel is pre-eminent.'

7. After that my grandfather Enoch took hold of me by my hand and raised me up, and said unto me: 'Go, for I have asked the Lord of Spirits as touching this commotion on the earth. And He said to me: "Because of their unrighteousness their judgment has been determined upon and shall not be withheld by Me for ever.

8. Because of the sorceries which they have searched out and learnt, the earth and those who dwell upon it shall be destroyed."

9. These-they have no place of repentance for ever, because they have shown them what was hidden, and they are the damned: but as for thee, my son, the Lord of Spirits knows that thou art pure, and guiltless of this reproach concerning the secrets.

10. He has destined thy name to be among the holy, and will preserve thee amongst those who dwell on the earth, and has destined thy righteous seed both for kingship and for great honours.

11. And from thy seed shall proceed a fountain of the righteous and holy without number for ever.

Chapter 66

1. After that he showed me the angels of punishment who are prepared to come and let loose all the powers of the waters which are beneath in the earth in order to bring judgement and destruction on all who dwell on the earth.

2. The Lord of Spirits gave commandment to the angels who were going forth, that they should not cause the waters to rise but should hold them in check; for those angels were over the powers of the waters.

3. And I went away from the presence of Enoch.

Chapter 67

1. In those days the word of God came unto me, and He said unto me: 'Noah, thy lot has come up before me, a lot without blame, a lot of love and uprightness.

2. And now the angels are making a wooden vessel, and when they have completed the task I will place My hand upon it and preserve it, and there shall come forth from it the seed of life, and a change shall set in so that the earth will not remain without inhabitant.

3. I will make fast thy seed before me forever and ever, and I will spread abroad those who dwell with thee: it shall not be unfruitful on the face of the earth, but it shall be blessed and multiply on the earth in the name of the Lord.'

4. He will imprison these angels who have shown unrighteousness in their burning vancy which my grandfather Enoch had formerly shown to me in the west among the mountains of gold and silver and iron and soft metal and tin.

5. I saw that valley in which there was a great convulsion and a convulsion of the waters.

6. When all this takes place, from that fiery molten metal and from the convulsion thereof in that place, there was produced a smell of sulphur, and it was connected with those waters, and that valley of the angels who had led astray burned beneath that land.

7. Through its valleys proceed streams of fire, where these angels are punished who had led astray those who dwell upon the earth.

8. But those waters shall in those days serve for the kings and the mighty and the exalted, and those who dwell on the earth, for the healing of the body, but for the punishment of the spirit; now their spirit is full of lust, that they may be punished in their body, for they have denied the Lord of Spirits and see their punishment daily, and yet believe not in His name.

9. In proportion as the burning of their bodies becomes severe, a corresponding change shall take place in their spirit for ever and ever; for before the Lord of Spirits none shall utter an idle word.

10. 10. For the judgement shall come upon them, because they believe in the lust of their body and deny the Spirit of the Lord.

11. Those same waters will undergo a change in those days; for when those angels are punished in these waters, these water-springs shall change their temperature, and when the angels ascend, this water of the springs shall change and become cold.

12. I heard Michael answering and saying: 'This judgment wherewith the angels are judged is a testimony for the kings and the mighty who possess the earth.'

13. Because these waters of judgement minister to the healing of the body of the kings and the lust of their body; therefore they will not see and will not believe that those waters will change and become a fire which burns for ever.

Chapter 68

1. After that my grandfather Enoch gave me the teaching of all the secrets in the book in the Parables which had been given to him, and he put them together for me in the words of the book of Parables.

2. On that day Michael answered Raphael and said: 'The power of the spirit transports and makes me to tremble because of the severity of the judgement of the secret, the judgement of the angels; who can endure the sever judgement which has been executed, and before which they melt away?'

3. Michael answered again, and said to Raphael: 'Who is he whose heart is not softened concerning it, and whose reins are not troubled by this word of judgment which has gone forth upon them because of those who thus led them out?'

4. It came to pass when he stood before the Lord of Spirits, Michael said thus to Raphael: 'I will not take their part under the eye of the Lord; for the Lord of Spirits has been angry with them because they do as if they were the Lord.

5.   Therefore all that is hidden shall come upon them for ever and ever; for neither angel nor man shall have his portion therein, but alone they have received their judgment for ever and ever.

Chapter 69

1.   After this judgment they shall terrify and make them to tremble because they have shown this to those who dwell on the earth.

2.   Behold the names of these angels. The first of them is Semjaza, the second Artaqifa, and the third Armen, the forth Kokabel, the fifth Turael, the sixth Rumjal, the seventh Danjal, the eight Neqael, the ninth Baraqel, the tenth Azazel, the eleventh Armaros, the twelfth Bartarjal, the thirteenth Busaseial, the fourteenth Hananel, the fifteenth Turel, and the sixteenth Simapesiel, the seventeenth Jetrel, the eighteenth Tumael, the nineteenth Turel, the twentieth Rumael, the twenty-first Azazel.

3.   And these are the chiefs of their angels and their names, and there chief ones over hundreds and over fifties and tens.

4.   The name of the first Jeqon: that is, the one who led astray the sons of God, and brought them down to the earth, and led them astray through the daughters of men.

5.   And the second was named Asbeel: he imparted to the holy sons of God evil counsel, and led them astray so that they defiled their bodies with the daughters of men.

6.   The third was named Gadreel: he it is who showed the children of men all the blows of death, and he led astray Eve, and showed the sons of men the weapons of death, the shields and the coat of mail, and the sword for battle, and all the weapons of death to the children of men.

7.   From his hand they have proceeded against those who dwell on earth from that day and for evermore.

8.   The forth was named Penemu: he taught the children of men the bitter and the sweet, and he taught them all the secrets of their wisdom. He instructed mankind in writing with ink and paper, and thereby many sinned from eternity to eternity and until this day.

9.   For men were not created for such a purpose, to give confirmation to their good faith with pen and ink.

10.   For men were created exactly like the angels, to the intent that they should continue pure and righteous, and death, which destroys everything, could not have taken hold of them, but through this their knowledge they are perishing, and through this power it is consuming me.

11.   The fifth was named Kasdeja: this is he who showed the children of men all the wicked smitings of spirits and demons, and the smitings of the embryo in the

womb, that it may pass away, and the serpent, and the smitings which befall through the noontide heat, the son of the serpent named Taba'et.

12. This is the task of Kasbeel, the chief of the oath which he showed to the holy ones when he dwelt high above in glory, and its name is Biqa.

13. This is he who requested Michael to show him the hidden name, that he might enunciate it in the oath, so that those might quake before that name and the oath who revealed all that was in secret to the children of men.

14. This is the power of the oath, for it is powerful and strong, and he placed this oath Akae in the hand of Michael.

15. These are the secrets of the oath...and they are strong through this oath: the heaven was suspended before the world was created, forever.

16. Through it the earth was founded upon the water, from the secret recess of the mountains come beautiful waters, from the creation of the world and unto eternity.

17. Through that oath the sea was created, and as its foundation, He set for it the sand against the time of anger, and it dare not pass beyond it from the creation of the world unto eternity.

18. Through that oath are the depths made fast, and abide and stir not from their place from eternity to eternity.

19. Through that oath the sun and moon complete their course, and deviate not from their ordinance from eternity to eternity.

20. Through that oath the stars complete their course, and He calls them by their names, and they answer Him from eternity to eternity.

21. In like manner the spirits of the water, the winds, all zephyrs and paths from all the quarters of the winds.

22. There are preserved the voices of the thunder and the light of the lightnings: and there are preserved the chambers of the hail and the chambers of the hoarfrost, and the chambers of the mist, and the chambers of the rain and the dew.

23. All these believe and give thanks before the Lord of Spirits, and glorify with all their power, there food is in every act of thanksgiving: they thank and glorify and extol the name of the Lord of Spirits forever and ever.

24. This oath is mighty over them and through it their paths are preserved, their course is not destroyed.

25. There was great joy amongst them, they blessed, glorified and extolled, because the name of that Son of Man had been revealed unto them.

26. And He set on the throne of His glory, the sum of judgment was given unto the Son of Man, He caused the sinners to pass away and be destroyed from off the face of the earth, and those who have led the world astray.

27. With chains shall they be bound, in their assemblage-place of destruction shall they be imprisoned, and all their works vanished from the face of the earth.

28. From henceforth there shall be nothing corruptible; for that Son of Man has appeared, and has seated Himself on the throne of His glory, and all evil shall pass away from before His face, and the word of that Son of Man shall go forth and be strong before the Lord of Spirits.

Chapter 106

1. And after some days my son Methuselah took a wife for his son Lamech and she became pregnant by him and bore a son.
2. His body was white as snow and red as the blooming of a rose, and the hair of his head and his long locks were white as wool, and his eyes beautiful.
3. When he opened his eyes, he lighted up the whole house like the sun, and the whole house was very bright.
4. And thereupon he arose in the hands of the midwife, opened his mouth, and conversed with the Lord of Righteousness.
5. And his father Lamech was afraid of him and fled, and came to his father Methuselah, And he said unto him: 'I have begotten a strange son, divers from and unlike man, and resembling the son of the God of heaven; and his nature is different and he is not like us, and his eyes are like the rays of the sun, and his countenance is glorious.
6. And it seems to me that he is not sprung from me but from the angels, and I fear that in his days a wonder may be wrought on the earth.

Chapter 7

12.17 a.m. 1 Jan 09

Called by a New Name

AT AN EARLY AGE, approximately during the summer of, the second time of taking the first grade. Two events took place in my life that signaled the beginning of the change of things in my life.

We lived in Houston, near the far end of a culdesac street called Berglane, on the right hand side of the street, we as kids called it "Bird lane", in the Acre Homes area.

'While sitting at the table having lunch with my brothers, all was going as usual. I was in my spot sitting at the end of the table facing the front door to the out side, which would be facing east. The front door was open and the screen door closed. It was a beautiful day outside, for we had just been called in for lunch, a few minutes earlier. Two of my brothers, Levett; we called him "Baybet", [my mother, whom we called "Muah" (our short version of Mother), would call him "Cheese"], was sitting at my left-hand side; he is a year younger than I am. And Rondale, who is two years younger, was sitting at my right hand side. My oldest brother Leversal was sitting at the other end of the table. "Bicell", as we called him, is around four or five years older than me. He is a Williams, and my other brothers and I are Chambers. And my little brother Reshunn, whom we simply called "Shunn", was sitting in a highchair, eating his food with both hands as usual, and making nothing but a mess, and sucking on the meat he was eating, typical toddler. Everybody was eating, forks and spoons clicking all the while against plates and everybody talking at the same time, it was some noise. In the middle of a half of mouth full of food and chewing, I heard a very masculine voice speak in a volume that was well above the commotion going on! "Andre..." this voice said, causing me to look up and at everyone in a rapid succession, I said, "What?", still looking at everyone, expecting an answer from some one. Then realizing that the voice did not match anyone sitting at the table, I asked outloud again, "Who called me? What you want?",

69

then, everybody said they didn't call me. I got up in kind of a hurry, and went to the front door and opening it I looked around outside to see if any body was out there. Nothing, not a soul in sight. Then turning back, I went into the backroom past the table to the two rooms in the back that are separated by the bathroom. Looking to the left, into our room as I went to the back, I looked just to see if their would be anyone there, although I knew that that idea would not be possible, seeing that there is only two screened windows and no outside door, I went to the room on the right, stopping at the door. I saw Muah folding clothes and watching a soap opera on the TV, but I saw no men on the screen. And then I looked and saw my baby sister Janice lying on the bed asleep near her. I watched Muah watch the TV for a second and then asked, 'Muah, did you call me?' She said, 'No Crebet, (for she called me that because of the character on "Bewitched" who was known as Mr. Krabbet, she thought that his demeanor reminded her of me.), 'I'm just watching TV, y'all finished eating? If y'all is, clean up the table.' 'No ma'am, we're not done yet, I heard somebody call me and I didn't know who it was.' She said something to the effect of – don't worry about it…as I went back to eat, although I was now moving at a more slower pace, due to the puzzling effect of what I was thinking. I was pondering the way the pronunciation of the name sounded coming from the voice that I had heard. Because everybody in my family called my name with the "An" sound in stead of the "Un" sound, because in that name, it sounds like 'Undre'. After a few minutes, I was back into the same mode as everyone else. Eating and everybody carrying on conversations at the same time again.

With what seemed about a week later, I was up in the top bunk bed wrapped up in a blanket taking me an afternoon nap, when suddenly I rolled out of bed, but not knowing it. All of a sudden I opened my eyes and was at the ceiling looking down at myself lying on the floor still wrapped in the blanket. I was in a calm state of mind as I watched myself, and I could see that I had banged my head on the dresser and the floor. Muah and Bicell soon discovered my lifeless body and I could see that they were getting pretty upset as they tried to revive me. The blood from my head was making them start to panic. But I was in a surprisingly happy frame of mind, and I was just about to call out their name, when I felt my feet being pulled down with the same type of force that a magnet would have, an irresistible type of an attraction. That's when I heard their voices desperately trying to awake me, opening my eyes in wide surprise, excitedly I began to tell them, 'I was looking at y'all from up at the ceiling! I heard y'all trying to wake me up! I was about to call y'alls names when it felt like my feet were being pulled down to the ground! I was up at the ceiling looking at y'all!' With a silent and astonished stare, they looked down at me, with their eyebrows raised in amazement! Then they both began to speak at the same time saying things like – "Boy you're alright, you was just dreaming, but we don't know why you on the floor! Get up, you're getting blood on everything, your head is bleeding!" I felt no pain and had no fear, that is, until I reached up and touched my head and looked at my hand and saw all the blood, and that's when the pain, the screaming and crying began! But I never forgot the feeling and the view that I had witnessed.

For as long as I could remember, our family was always in church every Sunday for Sunday school, morning service and evening service. Most Wednesdays we were there for prayer service and Thursdays for choir rehearsals. In about the eight grade we would find ourselves at lodge meetings on Saturdays, after we were initiated at the Masonic and Eastern Star Hall. Some times these meetings were held at other lodges in places like Dallas, Ft. Worth and other places out in the country. So, of course you can quess that my brothers and I were pretty bored and disappointed, especially because we had to miss our fun time that a Saturday would bring. It was around that time that I began to sneak and read books at home that I was told not to read. It seemed to me that there must have been something in them that I just had to see, else, why would they say don't read them. When they were away I would get one of the books and read for as long as possible, some times for thirty minutes to an hour. Amazing things about rituals, knowledge and most surprisingly, things about Jesus when he was a child. Things like when He made sparrows out of clay and clapped His hands and they came to life and flew away. Soon, I was full of questions about God and about why we follow the things taught us from an early age that no one questions. I remember watching "Good Times" one time and Michael was questioning the existence of God and his mom was saying things to the effect of – 'Because He just does exist!' and Michael responded by putting a pencil on the table and saying, 'There are two pencils here!' and his mom would reply, 'There is only one pencil there!' and he would point out how that is the way people are made to think without questioning, 'why?' I also began to question the same way. I even used that way of rationing with my mother before I began to question the ministers and teachers at other churches that us teenager and kids were going to on the church bus to white churches. At Turnpike Church of Christ I would debate with the teachers about subjects like, 'Why do people go to church on Sundays, how do they know that the Sabbath day was on a Sunday, what if it's on a Tuesday or something?' and subjects like that. Most times the back and fourths would be so interesting that the whole class would get involved in the conversation, which would basically change or eliminate the subject that we were suppose to study. But the teachers and most of the students really enjoyed the depth of these discussions. At the Shady Grove church, some of us received baptism. A few weeks later there was a lady there that seemed kind of strange to us in some sort of way that we couldn't quite put our 'finger on'. She didn't speak to any one, as though she couldn't talk, but we seemed to know that she was able to speak. During the service, she was introduced as a Prophet, and had people line up to get a prophecy written to them. I had to see what she would say about me. I can't remember everything she wrote because over the years, that paper got misplaced somewhere, but I may still have somewhere that

I just can't find it. But I do remember it saying that 'That He sees my desire to please Him and that the Holy Spirit would bubble up within me all my life. And that He will be with me always.' Not long after that I was baptized again at an apostolic church, because I wanted to make sure that I had it right. Not long after that I was anointed with heavy olive oil while a blessing was pronounced over me by a really deep group of people that I don't think that I ever saw again. Shortly after that, I was home praying and listening to R.W. Shambach on a live Christian radio program as they were casting out demons over in Dallas, and being in Grand Prairie, it seemed in a frightening way that I could feel a lot of spiritual movement flowing from that direction, it was chilling, but praying brought a calm reassurance over me and strength and bravery seemed to glow from within me.

Maybe it was about three years later, after spending a lot of time taking it upon myself to learn as much about the Holy Bible that I could, that I found it kind of hard to still able to blend in with others who were around my age. It was a mentally conflicting time in my life. I had a strange dream that bothered my mind. In this dream I was in what seemed to be a one-room apartment. The room was fairly dark except for the white glow that came from the kitchen area, it was to the right side of the room and a small dinner table with one chair facing east, but the light was not on. I had the understanding that Someone was in there as if cooking or something, but I wasn't sure, but I knew as if by instinct. I was sitting on an army style cot with my hands clasped, right hand over left fist and my elbows on my knees. I was thinking, but using no words in my mind, but comprehensive, nonetheless. I was facing the window which faced to the east, the blinds were closed and there was only one door to the outside which was to the left of the window, it faced north, and was closed and it's blinds were closed also. I stood and walked to the window and slightly lifted one of the blades to look out. It was like looking at the ocean and the sky touch at the end of the horizon and there were no buildings except the row to either side of my apartment. For as far as my eyes could see, all I saw were army men, in rank and files. Then, one of the soldiers broke rank and stepped forward a few steps towards the direction of my apartment turned to his left went a few feet, turned right and took two steps and began to talk to one of the upper ranked officers. After about twenty seconds or so, he saluted and turned and ran up to my door. As he was about to climb the few stairs from the street to my door, I turned towards my cot and stood as Jesus was sitting at the table. Still no words were exchanged, but I had the feeling of, "whose side am I on?" As I thought that, there was a knock at the door. I was only watching Jesus with my periphery vision, with my head slightly lowered, as was His head as He sat. At that point, I raised my head defiantly and turned towards the door ready to take on every one in that army, because I confidently knew whose side I was on. I was ready for battle, time to fight for the Lord! Another knock on the door, as I reached for the doorknob, prepared to speak and act in the defense of Christ; I could feel that He was feeling confident about my decision to protect and stand up for Him, then I woke up.

5:23 a.m. 1 Jan 09

During the summer of 1980, my brother, Rondale and I were baptized, for me it was the third time, just to make absolutely sure that I had done it the right way, I did not want to leave nothing to chance. I saw in a deep dream, that seemed for the life of me to be actually happening, he and I were walking on a side walk and talking about the things that were going on, things that really had nothing to do with anything pertaining to the Bible or religion, just teenagers stuff. It was almost completely nighttime and lights were on all over town as usual and the last few birds were flying to their nests. The sky was clear without a cloud anywhere and the stars were shining. As we proceeded I saw out of the corner of my right eye, something moving and glowing. So looking to my right in order to see what had caught my attention and I saw coming over the horizon, an extremely large object flying high in the sky, probably at the same height of an aircraft cruising about 35000 feet, but the object that I saw was about what seemed to be 1000 ft. tall and in the shape of the cross. It was golden in color and a slightly clear golden flame was around it, but the flame did not look as if it moved-but it also was not stationary and it trailed from the center of the cross in a straight line from it past the horizon, appearing as though it would make a perfect circle when it meets up with its starting point. I yelled for Rondale to look at what I was seeing, excitedly he replied, 'What's them glowing thangs flying up to the line?!', to which I was about to reply that I didn't know, this was just as the cross was about to fly overhead, although directly under it would have been about twenty miles away to our right, well now our left since we had stopped and turned back in the direction we had just come from to see what was going on. As I was about to speak, suddenly my eyes widen in surprise as I began to be lifted off the ground. I looked back at Rondale who was about 12 ft. below me now and said, 'Come on, this is great, come on!!'. He was shaking his head in a frightened 'NO' fashion, backing up, looking scared and eyes as big as golfballs. As I was getting father away, I had the felling as if the knowledge was placed in my mind that he would be following me up before long. At this point I looked at the cross as it flew by and saw that none of the glowing teardrop shaped images that were rising from the ground flying directly into it, but all were attaching themselves to the trailing flame. Inside the ones that were fairly close to me I could see people singing, or praying, or laughing excitedly at the experience of flying. I was feeling ecstatic about the feeling myself and experimented by rolling and flipping as I flew up. Now I was about 8,000 ft. up and getting closer to the beautiful golden flames which were now about three hundred ft. in diameter, when I looked back down to see if I saw my brother coming up yet and to see if any one else that I knew was flying also. Looking in both directions of the flight of the cross, I saw many rising golden teardrops, but I knew that the numbers were small compared to the number of people that were not rising. The whole experience was strangely overwhelming and the air was very warm, but pleasant. The whole time seemed to have taken about 5 minutes from the ground to the point of 1,000 ft. away from merging with the flame. As I was about to merge, I awoke. That day, I told my brothers about the dream and they were puzzled to its meaning as I was, but I kink of knew that it meant that it was a view of the catching up, or as most folks know it as, the Rapture. I just wish that I knew about when it will happen, because I am sooooo ready to go!

Chapter 8

The Gnostic Gospels

DURING THE YEAR 1945, a discovery was made in a cave by a shepherd, as he prepared to enter, he threw stones into it in order to make sure that there were no wild animals within it before he entered. While listening for the stone to land he heard it crash into what sounded like a clay pot breaking. Seeing no animals trying to escape he entered and attempted to find the source of the crash. There he found the broken jar and saw others around and near it. Upon investigating he found ancient writings in each of the jars. He took some home and showed his mother and since they were rather poor, she saw no other use for them than to use them as fuel for the fire, imagine what was burned and lost to the world. Some he kept which ended up in the hands of an antique dealer and over the passage of time into the hands of historians, professors, antique libraries and etc. These documents were found near a place called Nag Hammadi, and have since been the subjects of many great debates. I personally would love to be able to have copies of a few that I have only heard of and one that I had the opportunity to only read briefly, that one being "The Gospel of Mary of Magdala", the others being "The Gospel of Peter", "The Battle between the Children of the Light and the Children of the Darkness" and "The Gospel of Wisdom".

Here I will show you three gospels; The Gospel Of Thomas, (please under stand that in those days the name Thomas was a nick-name, which meant 'Twin', in other words, he looked just like Jesus). For it is known but not taught to the masses that he was the youngest brother of Jesus, of which he had two, Simon was next after Jesus. Also to be presented is The Gospel of Phillip and The Gospel of Truth.

Before getting into those three gospels, I will show you a few excerpts from "The Gospel of the Egyptians" and "The Exegesis on the Soul", exegesis means interpretations.

The Gospel of the Egyptians

Salome said, "How long will men die?"

[Salome is the older stepsister of Jesus, of which there were two, the younger name was Mariam, or in other words, Mary]

The Lord replied, "As long as you women bring forth."

[Referring to Genesis 3:16]

Salome replied, "I did well, then, by not bringing forth."

The Lord said, "Eat every plant, but do not eat the one which contains bitterness." [Referring to Genesis 2: 16-17 & 3:2-3]

Salome asked when what she was inquiring would be known.

The Lord said, "When you trample on the garment of shame, and when the two become one, and the male with the female neither male nor female.

The Exegesis on the Soul

Wise men of old gave the soul a feminine name. Indeed she is female in her nature as well. She even has a womb. As long as she was alone with the father, she was a virgin and in form androgynous. But when she fell down into a body and came to this life, then she fell into the hands of robbers. And the wanton creatures passed her from one to another and penetrated her. Some made use of her through rape, while others did so by seducing her with a gift. In short, they defiled her, and took her virginity. And in her body she prostituted herself and gave herself to one and all, considering each one she was about to embrace to be her husband.

When she had given herself to wanton, unfaithful adulterers, so that they might make use of her, then she sighed deeply and repented. But even when she turns her face from those adulterers, she runs to others and they compel her to live with them and render service to them upon their bed, as if they were her masters. Out of shame she no longer dares to leave them, whereas they deceive her for a long time, pretending to be faithful, true husbands, as if they greatly respected her. And after all this they abandon her and go. When she perceives the straits she is in and weeps before the Father and repents, then the Father will have mercy on her and he will make her womb turn from the external domain and will turn it again inward, so that the soul will regain her proper character.

When the womb of the soul, by the will of the Father, turns itself inward, it is baptized and is immediately cleansed of the external pollution which was pressed upon it, just as garments, when dirty, are put into the water and turned about until their dirt is removed and they become clean. And so the cleansing of the soul is to regain the newness of her former nature.

From heaven the Father sent her – her man, who is her brother, the firstborn. Then the bridegroom came down to the bride. Since that marriage is not like the carnal marriage, those who are to have intercourse with one another will be satisfied with that intercourse. And as if it were a burden they leave behind them the annoyance of physical desire. When they unite in the bridal chamber, they become a single life. For they were originally joined to one another when they were with the Father before the woman led astray the man, who is her brother. This marriage has brought them back together again and the soul has been joined to her true love.

Now it is fitting that the soul regenerates herself and become again as she formerly was. The soul then moves of her own accord. And she received the divine nature from the Father for her rejuvenation, so that she might be restored to the place where originally she had been. This is the resurrection that is from the dead. This is the ransom from captivity. This is the upward journey of ascent to heaven. This is the way to ascend to the Father. Then when she becomes young again she will ascend, praising the father and her brother, by whom she was rescued. Thus it is by being born again that the soul will be saved.

The Gospel of Thomas

These are the secret sayings which the living
Yeshua has spoken and Didymos Judas Thomas inscribed.

1.   And He spoke: Whoever finds the interpretation of these sayings shall not taste death.

2.   Yeshua says: Let him who seeks not cease seeking until he finds, and when he finds he shall be troubled, and when he has been troubled he shall marvel and he shall reign over everyone and find repose.

3.   Yeshua says: If those who would lead you, say to you: 'Behold, the Sovereignty is in the sky!' then the birds of the sky would precede you. If they say to you: 'It is in the sea!' then the fish would precede you. But the Sovereignty exists within you and it exists without you. Those enlightened by the Holy Spirit are drawn by the Most High to Himself, opening their spiritual eyes, then you shall know that you are the sons of the Living Father. Yet if you do not recognize yourselves then you are impoverished and you are poverty.

4.   Yeshua says: The person old in days will not hesitate to ask a little child of seven days concerning the place of life – and he shall live. For many who are first shall become last, and they who are last shall become first. And they shall become a single unit.

5.   Yeshua says: Recognize Him in front of thy face, and what is hidden from thee shall be revealed to thee. For there is nothing concealed which shall not be manifest and none under the earth which shall not be raised.

6.   His disciples asked Him, they say to Him: 'How do Thou want us to fast, and how shall we pray? And how shall we give alms, and what diet shall we maintain?' Yeshua says: Do not lie and do not practice hate – for everything is revealed before the face of the sky. For there is nothing concealed that shall not be manifest, and there is nothing covered that shall remain without being exposed.

7. Yeshua says: Blessed be the lion which the human eats – and the lion shall become human. And accursed be the human which the lions eats – and the human shall become lion.

8. And He says: The Kingdom is like a wise fisherman who cast his net into the sea. He drew it up from the sea full of small fish. Among them he found a large good fish. That wise fisherman, he threw all the small fish back into the sea, he chose the large fish without hesitation. Whoever has ears to hear, let him hear!

9. Yeshua says: Behold, the sower came forth – he filled his hand, he threw. Some indeed fell upon the road – the birds came, they gathered them. Others fell on the bedrock – and they did not take root down into the soil, and did not sprout grain skyward. And others fell among the thorns – they choked the seed, and the worm ate them. And others fell upon the good earth – and it produced good fruit up toward the sky, it bore 60-fold and 120-fold.

10. Yeshua says: I have cast fire upon the world – and behold, I guard it until it is ablaze.

11. Yeshua says: This sky shall pass away, and the one above it shall pass away. And the dead are not alive, and the living shall not die. In the days when you consume the dead, you transform it to life – when you come into the light, what will you do? On the day when you were united, you became separated – yet when you have become separated, what will you do?

12. The disciples say to Yeshua: We know that thou shall go away from us. Who is it that shall be Rabbi over us? Yeshua says to them: In the place that you have come, you shall go to Jacob the Righteous, for whose sake the sky and earth come to be.

13. Yeshua says to His disciples: Make a comparison to me, and tell me whom I resemble. Shimon Kefa says to him: Thou art like a righteous angel. Matthew says to him: Thou art like a philosopher of the heart. Thomas says to Him: Teacher, my mouth will not at all be capable of saying whom thou art like! Yeshua says: I'm not thy teacher, now that thou have drunk, thou have become drunken from the bubbling spring which I have measured out. And he takes him, he withdraws, he speaks three words to him: AHYH ASHR AHYH-I Am Who I Am. Now when Thomas comes to his comrades, they inquire of him: What did Yeshua say to thee? Thomas says to them: If I tell you even one of the words which He spoke to me, you will take up stones to cast at me – and fire will come from the stones to consume you.

14. Yeshua says to them: If you fast, you shall beget transgression for yourselves. And if you pray, you shall be condemned. And if you give alms, you shall cause evil to your spirits. And when you go onto any land to travel in the regions, if they receive you then eat what they set before you and heal the sick among them. For what goes into your mouth will not defile you – but rather what comes out of your mouth, that is what defile you.

15.   Yeshua says: When you see him who was not born of women, prostrate yourselves upon your faces and worship him – he is your Father.

16.   Yeshua says: People perhaps think that I have come to cast peace upon the world, and they do not know that I have come to cast conflicts upon the earth – fire, sword, war. For there shall be five in a house – three shall be against two and two against three, the father against the son and the son against the father. And they shall stand as solitaries.

17.   Yeshua says: I shall give to you what eye has not seen and what ear has not heard and what hand has not touched and what has not arisen in the mind of mankind.

18.   The disciples say to Yeshua: Tell us how our end shall be. Yeshua says: Have you discovered the origin, so that you inquire about the end? For at the place where the origin is, there shall be the end. Blessed be he who shall stand at the origin – and he shall know the end, and he shall not taste death.

19.   Yeshua says: Blessed be he who was before he came into being. If you become disciples to me and heed my sayings, these stones shall serve you. For you have five trees in paradise, which in summer are unmoved and in winter, their leaves do not fall – whoever is aquatinted with them shall not taste death.

20.   The disciples say to Yeshua: Tell us what the Sovereignty of the Heavens is like. He says to them: It resembles a mustard seed, smaller than all other seeds – yet when it falls on the tilled earth, it produces a great plant and becomes shelter for the birds of the sky.

21.   Mariam says to Yeshua: Whom are thy disciples like? He says: They are like little children who are sojourning in a field which is not theirs. When the owners of the field come, they will say: Leave our field to us! They take off their clothing in front of them in order to yield it to them and to give back their field to them. Therefore I say, if the householder ascertains that the thief is coming, he will be alert before he arrives and will not allow him to dig through into the house of his domain to carry away his belongings. Yet you, beware of the system – gird up your loins with great strength lest the bandits find a way to reach you, for they will find the advantage with you anticipate. Let there be among you a person of awareness – when the fruit ripened, he came quickly with his sickle in his hand, he reaped it. Whoever has ears to hear, let him hear!

22.   Yeshua sees little children who are being suckled. He says to his disciples: These little children who are being suckled are like those who enter the Kingdom. They say to Him: Shall we thus by becoming little children enter the Kingdom? Yeshua says to them: When you make the two one, and you make the inside as the outside and the outside as the inside and the above as the below, and if you establish the male with the female as a single unity so that the man will not be masculine and the woman not be feminine, when you establish eye in the place of an eye and a

hand in the place of a hand and a foot in the place of a foot and an image in the place of an image – then shall you enter the Kingdom.

23. Yeshua says: I shall choose you, one from a thousand and two from ten thousand – and they shall stand as a single unity.

24. His disciples say: Show us thy place, for it is compulsory for us to seek it. He says to them: Whoever has ears, let him hear! Within a person of light there is light, and he is illumines the entire world. When he does not shine, there is darkness.

25. Yeshua says: Love thy brother as thy soul, protect him as the pupil of thine eye.

26. Yeshua says: The mote which is in thy brother's eye thou see – but the plank that is in thine own eye thou see not. When thou cast the plank out of thine own eye, then shall thou see clearly to cast the mote out of thy brother's eye.

27. Yeshua says to them: Unless you fast from the system, you shall not find the Sovereignty of the Most High. Unless you keep the whole week as the Sabbath, you shall not behold the Father.

28. Yeshua says: I stood in the midst of the world, and incarnate I appear to them. I found them all drunk, I found none among them athirst. And My soul was grieved for the sons of men, for they are blind in their hearts and do not see that empty they came into the world and that empty they are destined to come forth again from the world. However, now they are drunk – when they shaken off their wine, then shall they rethink.

29. Yeshua says: If the flesh has come to be because of spirit, it is a marvel – yet if spirit because of the body, it would be a marvel among marvels. But I marvel at this, how this great wealth has inhabited this poverty.

30. Yeshua says: Where there are three gods, they are godless. Where there is only one, I say that I myself am with Him.

31. Yeshua says: No prophet is accepted in his own village, no physician heals those who know him.

32. Yeshua says: A city being built upon a high mountain and fortified cannot fall nor can it be hidden.

33. Yeshua says: What thou shall hear in thy ear proclaim to other ears from your rooftops. For no one kindles a lamp and sets it under a basket nor puts it in a hidden place, but rather it is placed upon the lampstand so that everyone who comes in and goes out will see its light.

34. Yeshua says: If a blind person leads a blind person, both together fall into a pit.

35. Yeshua says: It is impossible for anyone to enter the house of the strong and take it by force, unless he binds his hands – then he will ransack his house.

36. Yeshua says: Be not anxious in the morning about the evening nor in the evening about the morning, neither for your food that you shall eat nor for the garments that you shall wear. You are more superior to the flowers, which neither comb wool nor spin thread. When you have no clothing, what do you wear? Or who can increase your stature? He himself shall give to you garment.

37. His disciples say: When will thou appear to us, and when shall we behold thee? Yeshua says: When you take off your garments without being ashamed, and take your garments and place them under your feet to tread on them as the little children do – then shall you behold the Son of the Living One, and you shall not fear.

38. Yeshua says: Many times have you yearned to hear the sayings which I speak to you, and you have no one else from whom to hear them. There will be days when you will seek me but you shall not find me.

39. Yeshua says: The Pharisees and the theologians have received the keys of recognition, but they have hidden them. They did not enter, nor did they permit those to enter who wished to. Yet you – become astute as serpents and pure as doves.

40. Yeshua says: A vine has been planted without the Father, and as it is not viable it shall be pulled up by its roots and destroyed.

41. Yeshua says: Whoever has in his hand, to him shall more be given. And whoever does not have, from him shall be taken even the trifle, which he has.

42. Yeshua says: Be passers-by.

43. His disciples say to him: Who art thou, that thou say these things to us? Yeshua says to them: From what I say to you, you do not recognize who I be, rather you have become as the Jews – for they love the tree but hate its fruit, and they love the fruit but hate the tree.

44. Yeshua says: Whoever vilifies the Father, it shall be forgiven him. And whoever vilifies the Son, it shall be forgiven him. Yet whoever vilifies the Holy Spirit, it shall not be forgiven him – neither on earth nor in Heaven.

45. Yeshua says: They do not harvest grapes from thorns, nor do they gather figs from thistles – for they give no fruit. A good person brings forth goodness out of his treasures. A bad person brings forth wickedness out of his evil treasure which is in his heart, and he speaks oppressively – for out of the abundance of the heart he brings forth wickedness.

46. Yeshua says: From Adam until John the Baptist there is among those born of women none more exalted than John the Baptist – so that his eyes shall not be broken. Yet I have said that whoever among you becomes childlike shall recognize the Sovereignty, and he shall become more exalted than John.

47. Yeshua says: It is impossible for a person to mount two horses or to stretch two bows, and a slave cannot serve two masters – otherwise he will honor the one and offend the other. No person drinks vintage wine and immediately desires to drink new wine, and they do not put new wine into old wineskins lest they burst, and they do not put vintage wine into new wineskins lest it sour. They do not sew an old patch on a new garment because there would come a split.

48. Yeshua says: If two make peace with each other in this one house, they shall say to the mountain: Be moved! – and it shall be moved.

49. Yeshua says: Blessed be the solitary and chosen – for you shall find the Sovereignty. You have come from it, and unto it you shall return.

50. Yeshua says: If they say to you: 'From whence do you come?', say to them: 'We have come from the Light, the place where the Light has originated through Himself – He stood and He Himself appeared in their imagery. 'If they say to you: 'We are His Sons and we are the chosen of the Living Father.' If they ask you: 'What is the sign of your Father in you?', say to them: 'It is the movement with repose.'

51. His disciples say to Him: 'When will the repose of the dead occur, and when will the New World come?' He says to them: That which you look for has already come, but you do not recognize it.

52. His disciples say to Him: Twenty-four prophets proclaimed in Israel, and they all spoke within thee. He says to them: You have ignored the Living One who is facing you, and you have spoken about the dead.

53. His disciples say to Him: Is circumcision beneficial or not? He says to them: If it were beneficial, their father would beget them circumcised from their mother. But the true spiritual circumcision has become entirely beneficial.

54. Yeshua says: Blessed be the poor, for the Sovereignty of the Skies is yours.

55. Yeshua says: Whoever does not hate his father and his mother will not be able to become a disciple to me. And whoever does not hate his brothers and his sisters and does not take up his own cross in my way, will not become worthy of me.

56. Yeshua says: Whoever has recognized the system has found a corpse – and whoever has found a corpse, of him the system is not worthy.

57. Yeshua says: The Sovereignty of the Father is like a person who has good seed. His enemy came by night, he sowed a weed among the good seed. The man did not permit them to pull up the weed, he says to them: 'Lest perhaps you go forth saying: 'We shall pull up the weed', and you pull up the wheat along with it. For on the day of harvest the weeds will appear – they pull them and burn them.

58. Yeshua says: Blessed be the person who has suffered – he has found the life.

59. Yeshua says: Behold the Living One while you are alive, lest you die and seek to perceive Him and be unable to see.

60. Seeing a Samaritan carrying a lamb, entering Judea. Yeshua says to them: Why does he carry the lamb with him? They say to Him: So that he may kill and eat it. He says to them: While it is alive he will not eat it, but only after he kills it and it becomes a corpse. They say: Otherwise he will not be able to do it. He says to them: You yourselves – seek a place for yourselves in repose, lest you become corpses and be eaten.

61. Yeshua says: Two will rest on a bed – the one shall die, the other shall live. Salome says: Who art thou, man? As if sent by someone, thou laid upon my bed and thou ate from my table. Yeshua says to her: I Am He who is from equality. To Me have been given from the things of My Father. Salome says: I'm Thy disciple. He

replies: Thus I say that whenever someone equalizes he shall be filled with light, yet whenever he differentiates he shall be filled with darkness.

62. Yeshua says: I tell My mysteries to those worthy to ascertain My mysteries. What thy right hand shall do, let not thy left hand ascertain what it does.

63. Yeshua says: There was a wealthy person who possessed much money, and he said: I shall utilize my money so that I may sow and reap and replant, to fill my storehouses with fruit so that I lack nothing. This is what he thought in his heart – and that night he died. Whoever has ears, let him hear!

64. Yeshua says: A person had houseguests, and when he had prepared the banquet he sent his slave to invite the guests. He went to the first, he says to him: My master invites thee. He replied: I have some business with some merchants, they are coming to me in the evening, I shall go to place my orders with them – I beg to be excused from the banquet. He went to and they require me for a day, I shall have no leisure time. He came to another, he says to him: My master invites thee. He replied to him: My comrade is to be married and I must arrange another, he says to him: My master has invited thee. He replied to him: I have bought a house feast, I shall not be able to come – I beg to be excused from the banquet. He went to another, he says to him: My master invites thee. He replied to him: I have bought a villa, I go to receive the rent, I shall not be able to come – I beg to be excused. The slave came, he said to his master: Those whom thou have invited to the banquet have excused themselves. The master said to his slave: Go out to the roads, bring those whom thou shall find so that they may feast.

65. And Yeshua says: Tradesmen and merchants shall not enter the places of My Father.

66. He says: A kind person had a vineyard. He gave it out to tenants so that they would work it and he would receive its fruit from them. He sent his slave so that the tenants would give him the fruit of the vineyard. They seized his slave, they beat him – a little longer and they would have killed him. The slave went, and told it to his master. His master said: Perhaps they did not recognize him. He sent another slave – the tenants beat him also. Then the owner sent his son. He said: perhaps they will respect my son. Since those tenants knew that he was the heir of the vineyard, they seized him, they killed him. Whoever has ears, let him hear!

67. Yeshua says: Show me the stone which the builders have rejected – it is the cornerstone.

68. Yeshua says: Whoever knows everything but himself, lacks everything.

69. Yeshua says: Blessed be you when when you are hated and persecuted and find no place there where you have been persecuted.

70. Yeshua says: Blessed be those who have been persecuted in their heart – these are they who have recognized the Father in truth.

71. He says: Blessed be the hungry, for the stomach of him who desires shall be filled.

72. Yeshua says: When you bring forth that which is within you, this that you shall have shall save you. If you do not have that within you, this which you do not have within you will kill you.

73. Yeshua says: I shall destroy this house, and no one will be able to build it.

74. A man spoke to Him: Tell my brothers to divide the possessions of my father with me. He says to him: Oh man, who made me a divider? He turned to His disciples, He says to them: I'm not a divider, am I?

75. Yeshua says: The harvest is indeed plentiful, but the workers are few. Yet beseech the Lord that He send workers into the harvest.

76. He says: Lord, there are many around the reservoir, yet no one in the reservoir.

77. Yeshua says: There are many standing at the door, but the solitary are those who shall enter the Bridal-Chamber.

78. Yeshua says: The Sovereignty of the Father is like a merchant possessing a fortune, who found a pearl. That merchant was shrewd – he sold the fortune, he bought the one pearl for himself. You yourselves, seek for the treasures of God, which perishes not, which endures – the place where no moth comes near to devour nor worm ravages.

79. Yeshua says: I Am the Light who is above them all, I-Am the All. All came forth from Me and all return to Me. Cleave wood, there am I. Lift up the stone and there you shall find Me.

80. Yeshua says: Why did you come out to the wilderness – to see a reed shaken by the wind? And to see a person dressed in plush garments? Behold, your rulers and your dignitaries are those who are clad in plush garments, and they shall not be able to recognize the Truth.

81. A woman from the multitude says to Him: Blest be the womb which bore thee, and the breasts which nursed thee! He says to all: Blest be those who have heard the meaning of the Father and have kept it in truth. For there shall be days when you will say: Blessed be the womb which has not conceived and the breast which have not nursed.

82. Yeshua says: Whoever has recognized the system has found the body – and whoever has found the body, of him the system is not worthy.

83. Yeshua says: Let whoever is enriched become sovereign, and let whoever has power renounce it.

84. Yeshua says: Whoever is close to me is close to the fire, and whoever is far from me is far from the Sovereignty.

85. Yeshua says: The images are manifest to mankind, and the Light which is within them is hidden. He shall reveal himself in the imagery of the Light of the Father – and thus his image is concealed by His Light.

86. Yeshua says: When you see your reflection, you rejoice. Yet when you perceive your images which have come into being in your presence – which neither die nor manifest – to what extent will they depend upon you?

87. Yeshua says: Adam came into existence from a great power and a great wealth, and yet he did not become worthy of you. For if he had been worthy, he would not have experienced death.

88. Yeshua says: Foxes have their dens and the birds have their nests, yet the Son of Man has no place to lay His head for rest.

89. Yeshua says: Wretched be the body which depends upon another body, and wretched be the soul which depends upon their being together.

90. Yeshua says: The angels and the oracles shall come to you, and they shall bestow upon you what is yours. And you yourselves, give to them what is in your hands, and say among yourselves: On what day will they come to receive what is theirs?

91. Yeshua says: Why do you wash the outside of the chalice? Do you not mind that He who creates the inside is also He who creates the outside?

92. Yeshua says: Come unto Me, for My yoke is light and My Lordship is gentle – and you shall find repose for yourselves.

93. They say to Him: Tell us who thou art, so that we may believe in Thee. He says to them: You scrutinized the face of the sky and of the earth – yet you do not recognize Him who is facing you, and you do not know to inquire of Him at this moment.

94. Yeshua says: Seek and you shall find. But those things which you asked me in those days, I did not tell you then. Now I wish to tell them, and you do not inquire about them.

95. Yeshua says: Give not what is sacred to the dogs, lest they throw it on the dungheap. Cast not the pearls to the swine, lest they cause it to become trampled and turn to rend you to pieces.

96. Yeshua says: Whoever seeks shall find. And whoever knocks, it shall be opened to him.

97. Yeshua says: If you have copper – coins, do not lend at interest – but rather give them to those from whom you will not be repaid.

98. Yeshua says: The Sovereignty of the Father is like a woman, she has taken a little yeast, she hid it in dough, she produced large loaves of it. Whoever has ears, let him hear!

99. Yeshua says: The Sovereignty of the Father is like a woman who was carrying a jar full of grain. While she was walking along a distant road, the handle of the jar broke, the grain streamed out behind her onto the road. She did not know it, she had noticed no accident. When she arrived in her house, she set the jar down – she found it empty.

100. Yeshua says: The Sovereignty of the Father is like someone who wishes to slay a prominent person. He drew forth his sword in his house, he thrust it into the

wall in order to ascertain whether his hand would prevail. Then he slew the prominent person.

101. His disciples say to him: Thy brethren and thy mother are standing outside. He says to them: Those here who practice the desires of My Father – these are my brethren and My mother. It is they who shall enter the Kingdom of my Father.

102. They show Yeshua a gold-coin, and they say to him: The agents of Caesar extort tribute from us. He says to them: Give the things of Caesar to Caesar, give the things of God to God, and give to Me what is Mine.

103. He says: Whoever does not hate his father and his mother in My way, shall not be able to become a discile to Me. And whoever does not love his father and his mother in my way, shall not be able to become a disciple to Me. For My mother bore Me, yet My true Mother gave me the life.

104. Yeshua says: Woe unto them, the Pharisees – for they are like a dog sleeping in the manger of oxen. For neither does he eat, nor does he allow the oxen to eat.

105. Yeshua says: Blessed be the person who knows in which part the bandits may invade, so that he shall arise and collect his weapons and gird up his loins before they enter.

106. They say to Yeshua: Come, let us pray today and let us fast. Yeshua says: Which then is the transgression that I have committed, or in what have I been vanquished? But when the Bridegroom comes forth from the Bridal-Chamber, then let them fast and let them pray.

107. Yeshua says: Whoever acknowledges father and mother, shall be called the son of a harlot.

108. Yeshua says: When you make the two one, you shall become Sons of Mankind- and when you say to the mountain: Be moved!, it shall be moved.

109. Yeshua says: The Sovereignty is like a shepherd who has 100 sheep. One of them went astray, which was the largest. He left the 99, he sought for the one until he found it. Having wearied himself, he said to that sheep: I desire thee more than the 99.

110. Yeshua says: Whoever drinks from My mouth shall become like Me. I Myself shall become him, and the secrets shall be manifest to him.

111. Yeshua says: The Sovereignty is like a person who has a treasure buried in his field without knowing it. And when he died, he bequeathed it to his son. His son did not know of it, he accepted that field, he sold it. And he came who purchased it – he plowed it, discovering the treasure. He began to lend money at interest to whomever he wishes.

112. Yeshua says: Whoever has found the system and been enriched, let him renounce the system.

113. Yeshua says: The sky and the earth shall be rolled up in your presence. And he who lives from within the Living One shall see neither death nor fear the

destruction of the wicked, for Yeshua says: Whoever finds himself, of him the world is not worthy.

114. Yeshua says: Woe to the flesh which depends upon the soul, woe to the soul which depends upon the flesh.

115. His disciples say to Him: When will the Sovereignty come? He says: It shall not come by expectation. They will not say: Behold here! Or: Behold there! But the Sovereignty of the Father is spread upon the earth, and Humans do not perceive it.

116. Shimon Kefa says to them: Let Miriam (the Magdalene) depart from among us, for women are not worthy of the life. Yeshua says: Behold, I shall entice her so that I make her male, in order that she herself shall become a living spirit like you males. For every female who become male shall enter the Sovereignty of the Heavens.

The Gospel of Philip

1. A Hebrew person makes a proselyte Hebrew, and they call him thus: a novice. Yet a novice does not make other novice. In truth, proselytes are as they are naturally and also influence others to heed that calling, but with others less inspired, it suffices to them that they shall be.

2. The slave seeks only to be set free, yet he does not seek after the estate of his master. Yet the son not only acts as a son, but also ascribes to himself the inheritance of the father.

3. Those who inherit the dead are themselves dead, and they inherit the dead. Those who inherit the living are alive, and they inherit both the living and the dead. The dead do not inherit anything. For how will the dead inherit? When the dead inherits the living, he shall not die but rather the dead shall instead live.

4. A nationalist does not die, for he has never lived so that he could die. Whoever has trusted the truth became alive – and this- one is in danger of dying a martyr's death, for he is alive since the day that the Christ came.

5. The system is contrived, the cities are constructed, the dead are carried out.

6. In the days when we were Hebrews we were orphans, having only our Mother the Holy Spirit. Yet when we became Messianics, the Father unites with the Mother.

7. Those who sow in the winter reap in the summer. The winter is the world, the summer is the other aeon. Let us sow in the world so that we will harvest in the summer. Because of this, it is appropriate for us not to be made to pray in the wintertime. What emerges from the winter is the summer. Yet if anyone reaps in the winter he will not harvest but rather uproot, as this method will not produce fruit. Not only does it not come forth in wintertime, but in the other Sabbath also his field shall be fruitless.

8. The Christ came! Some indeed he ransomed, yet others He rescued, yet for others He atoned. He ransomed the alienated, He brought them to Himself. And He rescued those who came to Him. These He set as pledges in His will. Not only when He appeared did He voluntarily lay down His soul, but since the day of the world's coming-to-be He placed His soul. Then at the time He desired He came earliest to reclaim her, since she was placed among the pledges. She had come to be under the bandits and they had taken her captive, yet he rescued her. He atoned for both the good and the evil in the world.

9. The light with the darkness, life with death, the right with the left are brothers one to another. It is not possible for them to be separated from one another. Because of this, neither is the good a good, nor are the evils an evil, nor is the life a life, nor is the death a death. Therefore each individual shall be resolved into his origin from the beginning. Yet those who have been exalted above the world are indissoluble, are eternal.

10. The names which have been given by the worldly – therein is a great confusion. Foe their hearts are turned away from the real unto the unreal. And he who hears the word 'God' does not think of the real, but rather he is made to think of the unreal. So also with the words 'the Father' and 'the Son' and 'the Holy Spirit' and 'the Life' and 'the Light' and 'the Resurrection' and 'the Convocation' and all the other titles-they do not think of the real, but rather they are made to think of the unreal. Moreover they learn the worldly reality of death. They are in the system, it only they consider real. If they were in eternity, they would not designate anything as a worldly evil nor would they be placed within worldly events. There is a destiny for them in eternity.

11. One single name they do not utter in the world - the name which the Father bestows upon Himself in the Son. This He exalts above every other name. For the Son will not become the Father unless the name of the Father was bestowed upon Him. This existing name they are indeed each made to think to himself, yet they speak it not. Yet those do not have it do not even think it. But the truth begets these words in the world for us. It would not be possible to learn it without words.

12. She alone is the truth. She makes the many, and concerning us she teaches this alone in love thru many.

13. The authorities desire to deceive humankind, because they perceived him being in a kinship to the truly good. So they took the word 'good', they applied it to the ungood so that thru words they might deceive and bind him within the ungood. And subsequently whenever grace is enacted to them, they are to be withdrawn from the ungood and be appointed in the good – as these know. For they desire to take the free person and keep him as a slave to themselves forever. There is empowerment given to humans. They do not want him to understand, so that they will become rulers over him. For if there is mankind, there is hierarchy.

14. Sacrifice began after Eden, and they offered up animals to the powers. Subsequently, they indeed offered them up alive, but when they were offered up they died. But the human was offered up dead to God, and he lived.

15. Before Christ came there was no bread in the world as there had been in paradise, the place where Adam was. There were many plants as nourishment for the animals, but it had no grain as food for humankind. So humans ate like the animals. But Christ came, the perfect person. He brought forth bread in Heaven so that humankind would be nourished with the food of humankind.

16. The authorities were thinking that by their own power and volition they accomplish what they do. Yet the Holy Spirit in secret was energizing everything thru them as she wished.

17. The truth is sown everywhere from the origin, and the multitudes see it sown. Yet few who see it reap it.

18. Some say that Miriam was impregnated by the Holy Spirit. They are confused, they know not what they say. Whenever was a female impregnated by a female? Miriam is the virgin whom no powers defile, great among the consecrations for the Hebrew Apostles and for the Apostolics. Whoever of the powers attempted to defile this virgin, none such powers defile themselves. And the Lord was not going to say 'My fathers in the heavens', unless indeed He had another father – but rather He said simply My Father.

19. The Lord says to the disciples: Angels indeed come into the house of the Father, but do not possess anything in the house of the Father nor take anything away.

20. Yeshua is a secret name, Christ is a revealed name. Thus Yeshua does not occur in any other languages, but rather His name is Yeshua as he is called. Yet His name Christ in Aramaic is Messiah, but in Ionian is Cristos. Altogether, it is in all the other languages according to each one's word for 'anointed'. The revealed Nazarene is the secret!

21. The Christ has everything within himself – whether human or angel or mystery, and also the Father.

22. Those who say to themselves that the Lord first died and then arose, are confused. For first He arose and then died. If someone does not first acquire the resurrection, he will die; for he is not really alive before God was transforming him.

23. No one will hide a precious valuable in something expensive, but oftentimes has something worth countless myriads been placed in something worth a pittance. Thus is the case with the soul – a precious thing has come to be in a lowly body.

24. Some are fearful lest they arise naked. Therefore they desire to arise in the flesh, and they do not know that those who wear the flesh are the denuded. Those others who are divested of the flesh are those who are clad in His Spirit.

25. Paul proclaimed that with 'flesh and blood will not inherit the Sovereignty of God'. What is this which shall not inherit? This which is upon us? Yet this is exactly what will inherit – that which belongs to Yeshua with His flesh and blood.

Therefore he says: Whoever shall not eat my flesh and drink My blood has no life within himself. What is His flesh? – it is the Logos. And His blood? – it is the Holy Spirit. Whoever has received these has food and drink and clothing. I disagree with those who say that flesh and blood shall not arise. Then these both are wrong: thou say that the flesh shall not arise, but tell me what will arise so that we may honor Thee; Thou say it is the spirit in the flesh and this light in the flesh, but this also is an incarnate saying. For whatever thou will say, thou do not speak apart from the flesh! It is necessary to arise in this flesh, as everything exists within it.

26. In this world they who wear garments of cloth are more valuable than the garments. In the Sovereignty of the Heavens the garments of fine linen are more valuable than those to whom they have been given by means of water and fire, which purify the entire place.

27. The revelations by means of revelation, the secrets by means of secrecy. Some things are kept secret by means of the revelations.

28. There is liquid in water, there is fire in Chrism.

29. Yeshua took them all by surprise. For He did not reveal Himself as He really was, but rather He reveals Himself as they would be able to perceive Him. He revealed Himself to them all and He revealed Himself to the great as great, He revealed Himself to the small as small, He revealed Himself to the angels as an angel and to humans as a human. Thus His logos concealed Him from everyone. Some indeed saw Him while they thought they were seeing themselves. But when He revealed Himself to His disciples in Glory upon the mountain He was not made small. He became great, but He also made the disciples great so that they would be capable of beholding Him made great.

30. He says today in the Eucharist: He who has mated the Perfect light with the Holy Spirit, mates also our angels with the images.

31. Do not disdain the lamb, for without Him it is impossible to see the door. No one divested will be able to enter unto the King.

32. The Sons of the Celestial Person are more numerous than those of the earthly person. If the sons of Adam are numerous although they surely die, how many more are the Sons of the Perfect Person – those who do not die but rather are continually born!

33. The Father creates a Son, but it is not possible for the Son himself to create a Son. For it is impossible for Him who is begotten Himself to beget. But rather the Son begets for Himself Brothers instead of Sons.

34. All those who are begotten within the system are begotten physically, and the others are begotten spiritually. Those begotten in His heart are sent there to humankind to guide them in the promise of eternal life which is above, with God.

35. The Logos comes forth from the mouth. And he who is nourished from the mouth shall become perfect. The perfect are conceived thru a kiss and they are born. Therefore we also kiss one another – to receive conception in our mutual grace.

36. There were three Miriams who walked with the Lord at all times: His mother and older sister and the Magdalene-she who is called His mate. Thus His human Mother, Sister and Mate is each called 'Miriam'.

37. 'Father' and 'Son' are single names, 'Holy Spirit' is a double name. For the Father and the Son are everywhere – above and below, secretly and manifestly. The Holy Spirit is the secret above within the manifestation below.

38. The Saints are served by the oppressive powers, for the latter are blinded by the Holy Spirit so that they think they are assisting a human when in fact they are working for the Saints. Because of this, a Disciple one day made request of the Lord for something worldly, he says to Him: Request of Thy Mother and she will give to thee from what belongs to another.

39. The Apostles say to the Disciples: May our entire offering obtain salt! They called grace 'salt' – without it no offering becomes acceptable.

40. Wisdom is barren without the Son – hence she is called His Mother. But in the place of salt, Wisdom called the Holy Spirit has many Sons.

41. Everything that the Father possesses belongs to the Son. And also He the Son, as long as he is small, the Father does not entrust to Him what is His. But when He matures, the Father bestows on Him all that He Himself has.

42. Those who are lost are also begotten by the Spirit, and they go astray thru her. Thus by this one breath, the fire both blazes and is extinguished.

43. Wisdom is one thing, and death is another. Wisdom is simply being prudent, yet the wisdom of death is itself dead. That which acknowledges death is called the minor wisdom.

44. There are animals which are subject to mankind, such as the calf and the donkey and others of this kind. There are others which are not subject, and live apart in the wilderness. Man plows the field by means of the animals that are subject, and from this he feeds both himself and the animals whether tame or wild. So it is with the Perfect Person – thru the powers that are subject He plows, providing for everything which exists. For because of this the entire place stands – whether the good or the evil, both the right and the left. The Sacred Spirit shepherds everyone and commands all the powers, both those who are subject and also those who are not subject and are isolated. For truly She continues always to control them above their own volition.

45. Adam was formed, and yet thou will not find his sons to be noble formations. If he were not formed but rather begotten, thou would find his seed to be noble. Yet for now he has been formed and he has begotten. What nobility is this?

46. Adultery occurred first, then murder. And Cain was begotten in adultery, for he was the son of the serpent. Therefore he became a manslayer just like his father, and he killed his brother. Yet every mating which has occurred between those who are dissimilar is adultery.

47. God is a dyer. Just as the good pigments which are called true then label the things which have been permanently dyed in them, so it is also with those whom God colors. Because His hues are imperishable, those who are tinted become immortal thru His coloring. Yet God immerses whomever He baptizes in an inundation of waters.

48. It is not possible for anyone to see anything of those that are established unless he becomes like them. Not as with the person who is in the world – he sees the sun without becoming a sun, and he sees the sky and the earth and all other things without being them. But in the truth it is thus – thou thyself saw something of that place, and thou came to be there. Thou saw the Spirit, thou became spiritual; thou saw the Christ, thou became christlike; thou saw the Father, thou shall become paternal. Thus in the eternal when thou see everything and though thou do not see thy self, yet thou see thy self in that realm. For what thou see, thou shall become.

49. Faith receives, love gives. No one can receive without faith, no one can give without love. Therefore we believe in order that indeed we shall receive, yet we love in order that we may truly give. Otherwise, if someone gives without love, he derives no benefit from giving.

50. Who ever has not received the Lord, is still of the Hebrews.

51. The apostles who preceded us called Him thus: Yeshua the Nazarite Messiah – that is Yeshua the Nazarite Christ. The last name is the Christ, the first is Yeshua, the middle is the Nazarite. Messiah has two references: both anointed and also measurement. Yeshua in Aramaic is the Atonement. Nazara is the truth, therefore the Nazarite is the true. Christ is the measurement, the Nazarene and Yeshua are the measured.

52. If the pearl is cast down into the mire it is not despised, nor if it is anointed with balsam oil is it more valued. But rather it has its great worth to its owner at all times. So it is with the Sons of God – whatever happens to them, they still have the great value to their Father.

53. If thou say 'I'm a Jew' – no one will be moved. If thou say 'I'm a Roman' – no one will be disturbed. If thou say 'I'm a Greek, a barbarian, a slave, a freeman' – no one will be troubled. If thou say 'I'm a Christic, (that is to say Christian) – everyone will tremble. May I receive in such a manner that nonbelievers will not be able to withstand hearing this name!

54. A god is a cannibal. Because of this, they sacrificed mankind to it. Before they sacrificed mankind, they were sacrificing animals. For these to which they sacrificed were not divinities.

55. Both vessels of glass and vessels of pottery come to be thru fire. But if glass vessels break they are recast, for they come to be by means of breath. Yet if pottery vessels break they are destroyed, for they come to be without breath.

56. A donkey going in a circle at a millstone did a hundred miles walking. When it was released it found itself still in the same place. There are also people who take many journeys but make no progress anywhere. When evening comes upon them, they discern neither city nor village, neither creation nor nature, neither power nor angel. In vain did the wretches toil!

57. The Eucharist is Yeshua. For in Aramaic they call him FARISATHA – this is, the outspread. For Yeshua came to crucify the world.

58. The Lord went into the dyeworks of Levi. He took 72 complexions, He threw them into the vat. He brought them all up white, and He says: This is how the Son of Mankind comes – as a dyer.

59. The wisdom which humans call barren is the Mother of the Angels. And the Mate of the Christ is Mariam the Magdalene. The Lord loved Miriam more than all the other disciples, and He kissed her often on her lips. The other disciples saw His loving Mariam, they say to him: Why do thou love her more than all of us? The Savior replied, He says to them: Why do I not love you as I do her?

60. While a blind person and one who sees are both in the dark, they do not differ from one another. But when the light comes, then he who sees shall behold the light yet he who is blind shall remain in the darkness.

61. The Lord says: Blest be he who was before he came into being. For he who is, both was and shall be.

62. The exaltation of mankind is not manifest but rather implicit. Because of this he dominates the animals which are stronger than him – who thus is great both manifestly and implicitly. And this gives to them their survival. Yet when mankind separates from them, they kill each other and gnash each other and devour each other, because they find no food. Yet when mankind cultivated the earth they found food.

63. If anyone goes down into the water and comes back up without having received, but says 'I'm a Christic', he has taken the name on loan. Yet if he receives the Holy Spirit, he has the gift of the name. He who has received a gift is not deprived of it, but he who takes a loan has it demanded from him.

64. This is how it is when someone exists in a mystery – the Sacrament of Marriage is grand. For the world is complex: the system is based upon mankind, yet mankind is based upon matrimony. Therefore contemplate the Pure Mating, for it has great power. Its imagery is in a defiling of bodies.

65. Among the unclean spirits there are male and female. The males indeed are those who mate with the souls inhabiting a female form, yet the females are those who unite with a male form – both thru disparity. And no one will be able to escape from these once they seize him unless he receives both male and female power

– which is the Bridegroom with the Bride. One receives them in the mirrored Bridal-Chamber. Whenever the foolish women see a male sitting alone, they leap upon him to carouse with him and defile him. So also the foolish men when they see a beautiful female sitting alone, they seduce her or coerce her in the desire to defile her. Yet if they see the man sitting together with his woman, the females cannot violate the man nor can the males violate the woman. So it is if the imagery and the angel are mated together, neither can anyone dare to violate the male or the female. He who comes forth from the world cannot be detained any longer merely because he used to be in the world. It is evident that he transcends both the yearning and the fear of the flesh. He is master over desire, he is more precious than jealousy. And if the multitude come to seize him and strangle him, how will he not be able to escape by the salvation of God? How can he fear them?

66. Many times there are some who come, they say: We are faithful, hide us Lord from unclean spirits and demons! But if they have the Holy Spirit, no unclean spirit will cling to them.

67. Do not fear the flesh, nor love it. If thou fear it, it will enslave thee. If you love it, it will devour and strangle thee.

68. One exists either in this world or in the resurrection or in the transitional regions. May it not occur that I be found in the latter! In this world there is good and evil. Its goods are not good and its evils are not evil. Yet there is evil after this world, which is truly evil and which is called the transition; it is death. While we are in this world it is appropriate for us to be begotten in the resurrection, so that we if we are divested of the flesh we shall find ourselves in the repose and not wander in the transition. For many go astray on the way. Thus it is good to come forth from the world before humankind transgresses.

69. Some indeed neither wish nor are able. Yet others if they wish gain no benefit, for they do not act correctly. For desire makes them transgressors. Yet not desiring righteousness conceals from them both the wish and the deed.

70. An apostolic in a vision saw some unbelievers who were in a house of fire, crying out in a fiery air, cast water in the flames. Though even the water in that place is aflame, and they declare to themselves: Even the water cannot save us, whatever we may wish! They received death as chastisement. This is called the outermost darkness. The enemy comes forth in water and fire.

71. The soul and the spirit of the Son of the Bridal-Chamber come forth in water and fire with light. The fire is the Chrism, the light is the fire. I do not mean this fire that has no form, but rather the other – whose form is white and which is made of beautiful light and which bestows splendor.

72. The truth does not come unto the system naked, but rather it comes in symbolic imagery. The world will not receive it in any other fashion. There is a rebirth together with a reborn imagery. It is truly appropriate to be reborn thru the

imagery. What is the resurrection with its imagery? – it is appropriate to arise thru the imagery. The Bridal-Chamber with its imagery? – it is appropriate to come into the truth. This is the restoration. It is appropriate to be born not only of the words 'the Father with the Son with the Holy Spirit', but also to be born of them themselves. Whoever is not begotten of them will have the name also taken from him. Yet one receives them in the Chrism which comes in the power of the cross, which the Apostles call: the right with the left. For this-one is no longer a Christic but rather a Christ.

73. The Lord did everything in a sacrament: a Baptism with a Chrism with a Eucharist with an Atonement with a Holy Bridal-Chamber.

74. He says: I came to make the outer as the inner and the below as the above. The other place is represented here in symbols. Wisdom, She is the one who is above. He who is revealed descended from there is called: he who is below. And he has the hidden that is there above him. For it is good that they say: the inner and the outer together with what is outside of the outer. Because of this, the Lord called destruction 'the outer darkness'. There is nothing outside of that. He says 'thy Father in secret'. He says 'Go into thy closet, shut thy door behind thee and pray to thy Father in secret'. This is He who is within them all. Yet He who is within them all is the fullness-beyond him there is nothing further within. This is what is meant by: He who is above them.

75. Before Christ some came forth. They are no longer able to enter into whence they came, and they are no longer able to exit from whither they went. Yet the Christ came. Those who had gone in he brought out, and those who had gone out he brought in.

76. In the days when Eve was within Adam, there was no death. When she separated from him, death came to be. If she again enters and he receives her, death will no longer be.

77. 'My God, My God, why oh Lord hast Thou abandoned Me? 'He said these words on the cross. For He rent asunder the entire place, having been begotten within the Holy Spirit by God.

78. The Lord arose from the death. He again became as he had been, but His flesh was made entirely perfect. He wore the flesh, but this perfect flesh is the true flesh. Yet earthly flesh is not true, but rather a mirror-image of the true flesh.

79. Let the Bridal-Chamber not be for the animals nor for the slaves nor the impure women, but rather it is the custom of free men with virgins.

(Note): This morning 24 January 09 at approximately 10am, my younger brother Levett (Babet) died in Denver Co. after falling into a comma last night.

80. Thru the Holy Spirit we are indeed born, yet we are reborn thru the Christ. In both we are anointed thru the Spirit – and having been begotten, we mate.

81. No one will be able to see himself either in water or in a mirror without light. Nor again will thou be able to see thyself in the light without water or a mirror. Therefore it is appropriate to baptize in both – in the light and the water. Yet the light is the Chrism.

82. There had been three vestibules for places of offering in Jerusalem – one open to the west called the holy, another open to the south called the Holy of the Holiness, the third open to the east called the Holy of the Holinesses where the high priest alone was to enter. Baptism is the holy vestibule, Atonement is the Holy of the Holinesses is the Bridal-Chamber. Baptism has the resurrection with the Atonement entering the Bridal-Chamber. Yet the Bridal-Chamber is more exalted than those. And thou will find nothing that compares with it.

83. Those who pray for Jerusalem pray in Jerusalem and they see Jerusalem. These are called the holies of the holinesses.

84. The sacred veil was torn in order to reveal the Bridal-Chamber, which is nothing but the imagery as that above. And the veil was torn from the top to the bottom, for it is appropriate for some from below to go above.

85. Those who are clothed in the Perfect Light – the powers can neither see them nor restrain them. Yet one shall be clothed with light in the sacrament of the Mating.

86. If the female had not separated from the male, she would not die with the male. Her separation was the inception of death. Therefore Christ came, so that He might overcome the separation that had obtained from the beginning and again mate the two. And to those who have died in the separation he shall give life by mating them. Yet the woman mates with her husband in the bridal-chamber. Those however who have mated in the Bridal-Chamber will no longer be separated. Because of this, Eve separated from Adam – because she did not mate with him in the Bridal – Chamber.

87. The soul of Adam came into being from a Spirit, and her Mate is the Christ. The Spirit bestowed upon Adam is his Mother, and is given to him in his soul. And yet because he was not mated together in the Logos, the dominant powers bewitched him. But those who mate with the Spirit in secret place are invited individually to the Bridal-Chamber, where they mate.

88. Yeshua revealed Himself by the River Jordan as the fullness of the Sovereignty of the Heavens who precedes the totality. Moreover he was begotten as a Son, moreover he was atoned, moreover he atoned.

89. If it is appropriate to tell a mystery, the Father of the totality mated with the Virgin who had come down – and a fire shone for him on that day. He revealed the great Bridal-Chamber. Thus His body came into being on that day. He came forth in the Bridal-Chamber as one who has issued from the Bridegroom with the Bride. This is how Yeshua established the essence of the totality. And it is appropriate for each one of the Disciples to enter into His repose.

90. Adam came into being thru two virgins – thru the Spirit and thru the virgin earth. Therefore Christ was begotten thru a virgin, in order to rectify the fall which had occurred in the beginning.

91. There were two trees in paradise – the one produces beasts, the other produces humans. Adam ate from the trees that produces beasts, becoming a beast he begot beasts. Because of this the beasts were then worshipped. Adam ate the fruit of that tree, and this bore many fruits of which were also eaten; humans begot humans and worshipped humans.

92. God creates mankind, yet mankind creates gods. This is how it is in the world – the humans create gods and they worship their creations. It would be more appropriate for the gods to worship the humans!

93. Thus is the truth regarding the deeds of mankind – those that come forth thru his power are therefore called works, but his creations are his sons who come forth thru His repose. Because of this, His power governs in His works, yet His repose is manifest in His sons. And thou will find that this also penetrates thru the imagery: this is the Mirrored Person – doing his works in his power, yet begetting his Sons in his repose.

94. In this world the slaves work for the free. In the Sovereignty of the Heavens the free shall serve the slaves: the Sons of the Bridal-Chamber shall serve the sons of marriage. The Sons of the Bridal-Chamber have a single name among them, the repose occurs to them mutually, they have no needs.

95. Contemplation of the imagery is the greatest knowledge of glories.

96. Those who go down into the water do not go down to death, for He atoned for those who have been baptized in His name. For He said: Thus we must fulfill all righteousness.

97. Those who say that they will first die and then arise are confused. If they do not first receive the resurrection while they live, they will receive nothing when they die. Thus it is said also of Baptism in stating that Baptism is great, for those who receive it shall live.

98. Phillip the Apostle says: Joseph the Craftsman planted a garden because he needed wood for his craft. He made the cross from the trees that he planted, and his heir hung on that which he had planted. His heir is Yeshua, yet the plant is the cross. But the tree of life is in the center of paradise, the olive tree from which the Chrism comes thru Him who is the resurrection.

99. This world devours corpses – everything which is eaten in it thereby dies. The truthful consumes the living – therefore no one nourished in the truth shall die. Yeshua came forth from that place and He brought nourishment from there. And to those whom He wished He gave life so that they would not perish.

100. God created a garden-paradise. Mankind lived in the garden; alive but not being made in God, hence their hearts gave desire to mankind. And this garden is the place where it will be said to me: Thou may eat this or nor eat that, according

to thy desire. In this place of the tree of knowledge gave life to mankind. The Torah is the tree. It has the capability to bestow the knowledge of god and evil. It neither stopped man from evil nor preserved him in the good, but rather it presupposed death for those who have ingested it. For death originated in His saying: Eat this but do not eat that.

101. The Chrism is Lord over Baptism. For from the Chrism we are called Christics, not because of the Baptism. And he is called the Christ because of the Chrism. For the Father anointed the Son, yet the Son anointed the Apostles, yet the apostles anointed us. He who is anointed has everything-he has the resurrection, the light, the cross, the Holy Spirit. The Father bestowed this upon him in the Bridal-Chamber, he received.

102. The Father was in the Son, and the Son in the Father. This is the Sovereignty of the Heavens!

103. Ideally did the Lord say: Some have entered the Sovereignty of the Heavens laughing, and they came forth rejoicing from the world. The Christic believer who went down into the water immediately came forth as lord over everything, because he not only considered this system a game but also disdained it for the Sovereignty of the Heavens. Therefore if he disparages it and scorns it as a game, he will come forth laughing.

104. Furthermore, this is how it is with the bread and the chalice and with the ointment – there is nonetheless another sacrament more exalted than these.

105. The system began in a transgression, for he who made it desired to make it imperishable and immoral. He fell away and did not attain his ambition. For there is no imperishability of the system, and there was no imperishability of him who has made the system. For there is no imperishability of things but only of Sons, and no one can obtain imperishability except by becoming a Son. Yet he who is unable to receive, how much more will he be unable to give!

106. The chalice of communion contains wine and water. It is prescribed as the symbol of the blood, over it thanks are given. And it is filled with the Holy Spirit, and it belongs to the completely Perfected Person. Whenever we drink this, we receive the Perfect Person.

107. The living water is a body. It is appropriate that we be clothed with the Living Person. Because of this, when he comes to go down into the water he undresses himself in order that he may be clothed with that.

108. A horse begets a horse, a human begets a human, a god begets a god. This is how it is with the Bridegroom within the Bride – the Sons come forth in the Bridal-Chamber. Jews did not likewise derive from the Greeks, and Gentiles do not derive from the Jews. Christics and these were called from the chosen generation of the Holy Spirit – the true person and the Son of Mankind and the seed of the Son of Mankind. This generation are named the true-ones in the world. This is the place where the Sons of the Bridal-Chamber are.

109. Mating in this world is the man upon the woman, the place of strength over weakness. In eternity the mating is something else in the likeness of this, yet it is called by these same names. Yet there is another Name which is exalted beyond all designated names, and which transcends force. For where there is force, there are those who are more precious than force.

110. The one is not, and the other is – but these are together the single unity. This is he who shall not be able to come unto me thru a heart of flesh.

111. Is it not appropriate for all those who possess the totality to understand themselves? Some indeed, who do not understand themselves, do not enjoy what they have. Yet those who do understand themselves shall enjoy it.

112. Not only will they be unable to seize the perfected person, but they will not be able even to see Him. For if they saw Him they would seize Him. In no other fashion will one be able to be begotten of this grace, unless he is clothed in the perfect Light and himself becomes one of the Perfect Lights. Being thus clad he shall enter into this perfection.

113. It is appropriate that we become perfect persons before we come forth from the world. Whoever has received everything without mastering these places will not be able to master that place, but rather he shall go to the transition as imperfect. Only Yeshua knows the destiny of that one.

114. The Saint is entirely holy, including his body. For if he receives the bread he sanctifies it, or the chalice, or anything else he receives he purifies. And how will he not purify the body also?

115. By perfecting the water of Baptism, Yeshua poured death away. Because of this, we indeed go down into the water yet we do not go down unto death, in order that we not be poured away into the spirit of the world. Whenever that breathes the winter comes, but when the Holy Spirit of the summer arrives.

116. Whoever recognizes the truth is free. Yet he who is free does not trangress, for 'he who transgresses is the slave of transgression.' The truth is the Mother, yet the recognition is the Concord. These to whom it is given not to transgress in the world are called free. These to whom it is given not to transgress have their hearts exalted by recognizing the truth. This is what liberates them and exalts them over the universe. Yet love edifies. He however who has been liberated thru recognition is enslaved by love for the sake of those who have not yet been able to be carried up to the freedom of recognition. Yet recognizing suffices to liberate them.

117. Love does not take anything, for how can it take anything when everything belongs to it? It does not say 'This is mine' or 'That is mine', but rather it says 'They are thine.'

118. Spiritual love is with fragrance. All those who are anointed with it enjoy it. As long as the anointed remain, those also enjoy it who stand beside them. But if they who are anointed with the Chrism withdraw and depart, those who are not

anointed but only stand alongside will still remain in their own miasma. The Samaritan gave nothing to the wounded man except wine and ointment – and it healed the wounds, for 'love covers a multitude of transgressions.'

119. Those whom the woman begets will resemble him whom she loves. If it is her husband they will resemble her husband, if it is an adulterer they will resemble the adulterer. Often, if there is a woman who sleeps with her husband by compulsion yet her heart is toward the adulterer and she mates with him and begets, then the one to whom she gives birth resembles the adulterer. Yet you who are with the Sons of God – love not the world but rather love the Lord, so that those whom you beget will not be made to resemble the world but rather will be made to resemble the Lord.

120. The human unites with the human, the horse unites with the horse, the donkey unites with the donkey. The species unite with their like-species. Thus in this manner the Spirit unites with the Spirit, the Logos mates with the Logos, and the Light mates with the Light. If thou become human then mankind will love thee, if thou become spiritual then the Spirit will mate with thee, if thou become meaningful then the Logos will unit with thee, if thou become enlightened then the Light will mate with thee, if thou transcend then the Transcendental will repose upon thee. But if thou become like a horse or a donkey or a calf or a dog or a sheep or any other animal outside and inferior, then neither mankind nor the Spirit no the Logos nor the Light nor those above nor those within will be able to love thee. They will be unable to repose in thy heart and they will not be thy heritage.

121. He who is enslaved against his own volition, will be able to be freed. He who has been liberated by the gift of his master, and has sold himself back into slavery, will no longer be able to be freed.

122. Cultivation in the world is thru four modes – crops are gathered into the barn thru earth and water and wind and light. And the cultivation by God is likewise thru four: trust and expectation and love and recognition. Our earth is trust in which we take root, the water is expectation thru which we are nourished, the wind is love thru which we grow, yet the light is recognition thru which we ripen.

123. Grace made all the earth to be made as in Heaven above. Blest be this immortal!

124. This is Yeshua the Christ – He beguiled the entire place and did not burden anyone. Therefore blest be a perfect person of this kind, for such is the Logos.

125. Ask us concerning Him, inasmuch as it is difficult uprightly to resemble His actions. How shall we be able to succeed in this magnificent task?

126. How will He bestow repose on everyone? First and foremost, it is not appropriate to aggrieve anyone – whether great or small, unbeliever or believer. Then, to provide repose for those who rest in the good. There are some whose privilege it

is to provide repose for those who are ideal. He who does good cannot of himself give repose to them, for he does not come of his own volition. Yet neither can he grieve them, for he does not oppress or distress them. But he who is ideal sometimes grieves them – not that he is thus grievous, but rather it is their own wickedness which causes them grief. Whoever is natural gives joy to him who is good – yet consequently some grieve terribly.

127. The master of an estate acquire everything – whether son or slave or dog or cattle or swine, whether wheat or barley or straw or hay or bones or meat or acorns. He was wise and knew the food of each. Before the sons he indeed set bread and olive-oil with meat, before the slaves he sets castor-oil with grain, before the cattle he sets barley with straw and hay, to the dogs he cast bones, yet before the swine he threw acorns and crusts of bread. So it is with the Disciple of God – if he is wise he is perceptive about the Discipleship. The bodily forms will not deceive him, but rather he will look to the disposition of the soul of each one in order to speak with him. In the world there are many animals made in human form – these he recognizes. To the swine indeed he will throw acorns, yet to the cattle he will cast barley with straw and hay, to the dogs he will cast bones, to the slaves he will give the elementary, to the Sons He will present the Perfect.

128. There is the Son of Mankind and there is the grandson of mankind. The Lord is the Son of Mankind, and the grandson of mankind is he who is created thru the Son of Mankind. The Son of Mankind received from God the power to create as well as to beget.

129. That which is created is a creature, that which is begotten is a child. A creature cannot beget, a child can create. Yet they say: The creature begets. But a child is a creature. Therefore a mans children are not his sons but rather God's.

130. He who creates, works manifestly and he himself is manifest. He who begets, acts in secret and is himself hidden from the imagery of others. He who creates indeed creates visibly, yet he who begets the Sons begets them in secret.

131. No one will be able to know on what day the man and the woman mate with each other, except themselves only. For marriage in the world is a mystery for those who have taken a wife. If the marriage of impurity is hidden, how much more is the Immaculate Marriage a true sacrament! It is not carnal but rather pure, it is not lustful but rather willing, it is not of the darkness or the night but rather of the day and the light. A marriage which is exhibited becomes a prostitution, and the bride has prostituted herself not only if she receives the semen of another man but even if she leaves the bedroom and is seen. She may only display herself to her father and mother and the comrade of the bridegroom and the sons of the bridegroom. To these it is given to enter daily into the bridal-chamber and to see her. Yet as for the others, let them yearn even to hear her voice and to enjoy her fragrance, and let them feed like the dogs from the crumbs that fall from the

table. Bridegrooms with Brides belong in the Bridal-Chamber. No one will be able to behold the Bridegroom with the Bride unless he becomes this.

132. When Abraham rejoiced at seeing what he was to see, he circumcised the flesh of the foreskin - showing us that it is appropriate to sever the flesh likewise of this world.

133. As long as the flesh is intact the entrails of the person are enclosed, the person continues to live. But if his entrails are exposed and he is disemboweled, the person will die. So also the tree sprouts and thrives as long as it roots is covered, but if its root is exposed the tree withers. Thus it is with everything in the world, not only with the manifest but also with the covert. For as long as the root of evil is hidden it remains strong; yet when it is recognized it decomposes and when it is exposed it perishes. This is why the Logos says 'Already the ax has reached the root of the trees!' It will not merely chop off, for that which is chopped off sprouts again. But rather the ax delves down underground and uproots. Yeshua pulled up the root of the entire place, yet the others had done so only in part. As for ourselves – let each one of us dig down to the root of the evil that is within him and pull up its root from out of his own heart. Yet it will be uprooted if we but recognize it. Yet if we are unaware of it, it takes root within us and produces its fruits in our hearts. It becomes master over us and we become its slaves. We are taken captive, and we are coerced into doing what we do not want and not doing what we do want. It is potent because we do not recognize it. While it is subliminal it indeed impels.

134. Ignorance is the mother of all evils and fears. Those things which came forth from ignorance neither existed nor exist nor shall exist in reality. Yet they shall be perfected when the entire truth is revealed. For the truth is like ignorance – while it is hidden it reposes within itself, yet when it is revealed it is recognized. It is glorious in that it prevails over ignorance and confusion and in that it liberates. The Logos says 'You shall know the truth!, the truth will set you free. Ignorance is slavery, recognition is freedom. By recognizing the truth we shall find the fruits of the truth within our hearts. By mating with it we shall receive our fulfillment.

135. At present we have the revelation of creation. They say that visible beings are strong and honorable yet the invisible are weak and contemptible. However the truth is that visible beings are weak and inferior yet the invisible are strong and honorable.

136. But the mysteries of the truth are revealed in symbolic imagery. Yet the Bedroom is hidden – it is the holy within the holiness.

137. The veil indeed at first concealed how God governs the creation. Yet when the veil is torn and the things within are revealed, then this house will be forsaken and desolate and yet moreover it shall be destroyed. Yet the whole Divinity shall depart from these places, never to re-enter, for it shall not be able to unite therein

with the light and with the fullness. But rather it shall enter into the holies of the holinesses, under the wings of the cross and in its arms.

138. This ark shall become salvation for us when the cataclysm of water overwhelms them.

139. If someone is in the tribe of the priesthood, he shall be allowed to enter within the veil with the high priest. Therefore the veil was not torn at the top only, else it would have been opened only for those who are higher – nor was it torn at the bottom only, else it would have been revealed only to those who are lower. But rather it was torn from the top to the bottom. Those who are above have opened to us who are below in order that we might enter into the secret of the truth.

140. This strengthening is truly excellent. Yet we shall enter therein by means of despised symbols and weaknesses. They are indeed humble by comparison with the perfect glory. There is a glory that surpasses glory, there is a power which surpasses power. Therefore the perfect have opened to us with the secrets of the truth. Moreover, the holies of the holinesses are revealed, and the bedroom has invited us within.

141. As long as evil indeed remains covert it is potent, not yet truly purged from the mist of the seed of the Sacred Spirit. They are enslaved by the oppression. Yet when the Perfect Light is revealed, then it will pour forth upon everyone and all those within it shall receive the Chrism. Then the slaves shall be freed and the captives atoned.

142. 'Every plant which My heavenly Father has not sown shall be rooted out. Those who are separated shall be mated and the empty shall be filled. Everyone who enters the Bedroom shall be born of the Light. For they are not begotten in the manner of the unrighteous marriages which are enacted by night, the fire of which blazes in the dark is extinguished. Yet the Sacraments of this Marriage are consummated in the day and the light. That day with its light never sets.

143. If anyone becomes a Son of the Bridal-Chamber, he shall receive the Light. If he does not receive it in these places, he will not be able to obtain it in the other place. He who receives the Light shall not be seen nor shall he be seized, nor shall anyone disturb such a one even if he socializes in the world. And furthermore, when he leaves the world he has already received the truth in the imagery. The world has become eternity, because the fullness is for him the eternal. And it is thus revealed to him individually – not hidden in the darkness or the night but rather hidden in a Perfect Day and a Holy Light.

The Gospel of Truth

1. The Gospel of Truth is joy for those who have received from the Father of truth the gift of recognizing him, thru the power of the meaning who comes forth from the fullness which is in the thought and mind of the Father. This is he who

is called the Savior – that being the name of the task which he is to do for the atonement of those who had been unacquainted with the Name of the Father.

2. Now the Gospel is the revelation of the hopeful, it is the finding of those who seek Him. For since the totality were searching for Him from whom they came forth- and the totality were within Him, the incomprehensible inconceivable, He who exist beyond all thought – hence unacquaintance with the Father caused anxiety and fear. Then the anxiety condensed like a fog so that no one could see.

3. Wherefore confusion grew strong, contriving its matter in emptiness and unacquaintance with the Truth, preparing to substitute a potent and alluring fabrication for truthfulness. But this was no humiliation for Him, the incomprehensible inconceivable. For the anxiety and the amnesia and the deceitful fabrication were nothing-whereas the established truth is immutable, imperturbable and of unadornable beauty. Therefore despise confusion! It has no roots and was in a fog concerning the Father, preparing labors and amnesia and fear in order thereby to entice those of the transition and take them captive.

4. The amnesia of confusion was not made as a revelation, it is not the handiwork of the Father. Forgetfulness does not occur under His directive, although it does happen because of Him. But rather what exists within him is acquaintanceship – this being revealed so that forgetfulness might dissolve and the Father be recognized. Since amnesia occurred because the Father was not recognized, thereafter when the Father is recognized there will be no more forgetting.

5. This is the Gospel of Him who is sought, which He has revealed to those perfected thru the mercies of the Father as the secret mystery: Yeshua the Christ! He enlightened those who were in darkness because of forgetfulness. He illuminated them. He gave them a path, and that path is the truth which He proclaimed.

6. Therefore confusion was enraged at Him and pursued Him in order to suppress and eliminate Him. He was nailed to a tree; He became the fruit of recognizing the Father. Yet it did not cause those who consumed it to perish, but rather to those who consumed it He bestowed a rejoicing at such a discovery. For He found them in Himself and they found Him in themselves – the incomprehensible inconceivable, the Father, this Perfect-One who created the totality, within whom the totality exists and of whom the totality has need. For He had held within Himself their perfection, which He had not yet conferred upon them all.

7. The Father is not jealous, for what envy could there be between Him and His members? For if the way of this aeon had prevailed they would not have been able to come unto the Father, who retains within Himself their fulfillment and bestows it upon them as a return to Himself with a recognition which is single in perfection. It is He who ordained the totality, and the totality is within Him and the totality had need of Him. It is like a person with whom some have been unacquainted, yet who desires that they recognize and love Him. For what did they all lack except acquaintance with the Father?

8. Thus He became a reposeful and leisurely guide in the place of instruction. The Logos came to the midst and spoke as their appointed teacher. There approached those who considered themselves wise, putting Him to the test - yet He shamed them in their vanity. They hated Him because they were not truly wise. Then after them all there also approached the little children, those who have the acquaintance of the Father. Having been confirmed, they learned of the face-forms of the Father. They recognized, they were recognized; they were glorified, they glorified. Revealed in their heart was the Living Book of Life, this which is inscribed in the thought and mind of the Father and which has been within His incomprehensibility since before the foundation of the totality. No one can take this Book away, because it was appointed for Him who would take it and be slain.

9. No one of those who trusted in salvation could have become manifest unless this book had come to the midst. This is why the Merciful and Faithful-One – Yeshua! – patiently endured the suffering in order to take this book, since He knew that His death would become life for many. Just as the fortune of the deceased master of the estate remains secret until his bequest is opened, so also the totality remained hidden so long as the Father of the totality was invisible – this – One thru whom all dimensions originate. This is why Yeshua appeared, clothed in that book.

10. He was nailed to a tree in order to publish the edict of the Father on the cross. Oh sublime teaching, such that he humbled Himself unto death while clad in eternal life! He stripped of the rage of mortality in order to don this imperishability which none has the power to take from Him. Entering into the empty spaces of terrors, He brought forth those who had been divested by amnesia. Acting with recognition and perfection, he proclaimed what is in the heart of the Father, in order to make wise those who are to receive the teaching. Yet those who are instructed are the living, inscribed in this book of life, who are taught about themselves and who receive themselves from the Father in again returning to Him.

11. Because the perfection of the totality is in the Father, it is requisite that they all ascend unto Him. When someone recognizes, He receives the things that are His own and gathers them to Himself. For he who is unacquainted has a lack – and what he lacks is great, since what he lacks is Him who will make him perfect. Because the perfection of the totality is in the Father, it is requisite that they all ascend unto Him. Thus each and everyone receives Himself

12. He pre-inscribed them, having prepared this gift for those who emerged from Him. Those whose names He foreknew are called at the end. Thus someone who recognizes has his name spoken by the Father. For he whose name has not been spoken remains unacquainted. How indeed can anyone hearken whose name has not been called? For he who remains unacquainted until the end is a figment

of forgetfulness and will vanish with it. Otherwise why indeed is there no name for those wretches, and why do they not heed the call?

13. Thus someone with acquaintance is from above. When he is called he hears and heeds and returns to Him who called, ascending unto Him. And he discovers who it is that calls him. In recognition he does the volition of Him who called. He desires to please Him, and granted repose he receives the Name of the One. He who recognizes thus discovers from whence he has come and whither he is going. He understands like someone who was intoxicated and who has shaken off his drunkenness and returned to himself, to set upright those things which are his own.

14. He has brought many back from confusion. He went before them into the spaces thru which their hearts had migrated in going astray due to the depth of Him who encompasses all dimensions without Himself being encompassed. It is a great wonder that they were within the Father without recognizing Him, and that they were able to depart unto themselves because they could neither comprehend nor recognize Him in whom they were. For thus his volition had not yet emerged from within Himself. For He revealed Himself so that all His emanations would reunite with Him in recognition.

15. This is acquaintance with the Living Book, whereby at the end He has manifested the Eternal-Ones as the alphabet of His revelation. These are not vowels nor are they consonants, such that someone might read them and think of emptiness, but rather they are the true alphabet by which those who recognize it are themselves expressed. Each letter is a perfect thought, each letter is like a complete book written in the alphabet of unity by the Father, who inscribes the Eternal-Ones so that thru His alphabet they might recognize the Father.

16. His wisdom meditates on the Meaning, His teaching expresses it, His acquaintance revealed it, His dignity is crowned by it, His joy unites with it, His glory exalted it, His appearance manifested it, His repose receives it, His love embodied it, His faith embraced it.

17. Thus the Logos of the Father comes into the totality as the fruit of His heart and the face-form of His volition. But He supports them all, He atones them and moreover He assumes the face-form of everyone, purifying them, bringing them back – within the Father, within the Mother, Yeshua of infinite kindness. The Father uncovers His bosom, which is the Holy Spirit, revealing His secret. His secret is His Son! Thus thru the compassions of the Father the Eternal-Ones recognize Him. And they cease their toil of seeking for the Father and repose in Him, recognizing that this is the repose.

18. Having replenished the deficiency, he dissolved the scheme. For the scheme is this world in which he served as a slave, and deficiency is the place of jealousy and quarreling. Yet the place of the unity is perfect. Since deficiency occurred because the Father was not recognized, thereafter when the Father is recognized

there shall be no deficiency. Just as with ignorance, when someone comes to know, the ignorance dissolves of itself – and also as darkness dissipates when the light shines – so also deficiency vanishes when perfection appears. Thus from that moment on there is no more scheme, but rather it disappears in the fusion of the unity. For now their involvements are made equal in the moment when the fusion perfects the spaces.

19. Each one shall receive himself in the unification and shall be purified from multiplicity into unity in acquaintanceship – consuming matter in himself like a flame, darkness with light, and death with life. Since these things have thus happened to each of us, it is appropriate that we think of the totality so that the household be holy and silent for the unity.

20. It is like some who move jars from their proper places to unsafe places, where they are broken. And yet the matter of the house suffered no loss but rather rejoiced, for those unsound jars were replaced by these which are fully perfect. This is the judgment which has come from above, like a doubled-edged sword drawn to cut this way and that as each one is judged.

21. There came to the midst the Logos, which is in the heart of those who express it. This was not a mere sound, but rather it was incarnate. A great disturbance occurred among the jars – for lo some were emptied, others were filled, some were supplied, others were overturned, some were cleansed, others were broken. All of the spaces quaked and were agitated, having neither order nor stability. Confusion was in anguish at not discerning what to do – distressed and lamenting and cropping hair from understanding nothing.

22. Then when recognition approached with all its emanations, this was the annihilation of confusion which was emptied into nothingness. The truth came to the midst, and all his emanations recognized and embraced the Father in truth and united with him in a perfect power. For everyone who loves the truth attaches himself to the Father with his tongue by receiving the Holy Spirit. The truth is the mouth of the Father, His language is the Holy Spirit joined to Him in truth. This is the revelation of the Father and His Self-manifestation to His Eternal-Ones. He has revealed His secret, explaining it all.

23. For who is the Existent-One, except for the Father alone? All dimensions are His emanations, recognized in coming forth from His heart like sons from a mature person who knows them. Each one whom the Father begets had previously received neither form nor name. Then they were formed thru His Self-Awareness. Although indeed they had been in His mind, they had not recognized Him. The Father however is perfectly acquainted with all the dimensions, which are within Him.

24. Whenever He wishes He manifests whomever He wishes, forming him and naming him. And in giving him a name, He causes him to come into being. Before they came into being, these assuredly were unacquainted with Him who

fashioned them. I do not say however that those who have not yet come into being are nothings – but rather they pre-exist within him who shall intend their becoming when he desires it, like a season yet to come. Before anyone is manifest the Father knows what He will bring forth. But the fruit that is not yet manifest neither recognizes nor accomplishes anything. Thus all dimensions themselves exist within the Father who exists, from whom they come forth, and who established them unto Himself from that which is not.

25. Whoever lacks root also lacks fruit, but still he thinks to himself: 'I have become, so I shall decease – for everything that earlier did not yet exist, later shall no longer exist. What therefore does the Father desire that such a person think about himself? 'I have been like the shadows and the phantoms of the night!' When the dawn shines upon him, this person ascertains that the terror which had seized him was nothing. They were thus unacquainted with the Father because they did not behold Him. Hence there occurred terror and turmoil and weakness and doubt and division, with many deceptions and empty fictions at work thru these.

26. It was as if they were sunk in sleep and found themselves in troubled dreams – either fleeing somewhere, or powerlessly pursuing others, or delivering blows in brawls, or themselves suffering blows, or falling from a high place, or sailing thru the air without wings. Sometimes it even seems as if they are being murdered although no one pursues them, or as if they themselves are murdering their neighbors since they are sullied by their blood.

27. Then the moment comes when those who have endured all this awaken, no longer to see all those troubles – for they are naught. Such is the way of those who have cast off ignorance like sleep and consider it to be nothing, neither considering its various events as real, but rather leaving it behind like a dream of the night. Recognizing the Father brings the dawn! This is what each one has done, sleeping in the time when he was unacquainted. And this is how, thus awakened, he comes to recognition.

28. How good for the person who returns to himself and awakens, and blest is he whose blind eyes have been opened! And the Spirit ran after him, resurrecting him swiftly. Extending Her hand to him who was prostrate on the ground, She lifted him up on his feet who had not yet arisen. Now the recognition which gives understanding is thru the Father and the revelation of His Son. Once they have seen Him and heard Him, He grants them to taste and to smell and to touch the beloved Son.

29. When He appeared, telling them about the incomprehensible Father, He breathed into them what is in the thought of doing His volition. Many received the Light and returned to Him. But the materialists were alien and did not behold His likeness nor recognize Him, although He came forth incarnate in form. Nothing obstructs His course – for imperishability is indomitable. Moreover He

proclaimed beforehand that which was new, expressing what is in the heart of the Father and bringing forth the flawless Logos.

30. Light spoke thru His mouth, and His voice gave birth to life. He gave to them the thought of wisdom, of mercy, of salvation, of the Spirit of power from the infinity and the kindness of the Father. He abolished punishment and torment, for these caused some who had need of mercy to go astray from His face in confusion and bondage. And with power He pardoned them, and He humbled them in acquaintanceship.

31. He became a path for those who had strayed, acquaintance for the unaware, discovery for those who seek, stability for the wavering, and immaculate purity for those who were defiled.

32. He is the shepherd who left behind the 99 sheep which were not lost, in order to go searching for this-one which had strayed. And he rejoiced when he found it. For 99 is a number that is counted on the left hand, which tallies it. But when 1 is added, the entire sum passes to the right hand. So it is with him who lacks the One, which is the entire right hand – he takes from the left what is deficient in order to transfer it to the right, and thus the number becomes 100. Now, the signification within these words is the Father.

33. Even on the Sabbath he labored for the sheep which he found fallen into the pit. He restored the sheep to life, bringing it up from the pit, so that you Sons of heart-understanding may discern this Sabbath on which the work of salvation must never cease, and so that you may speak from this day which is above, which has no night, and from the Perfect Light which never sets.

34. Speak therefore from your hearts, for you are this Perfect Day and within you dwells this abiding light. Speak of the truth with those who seek it, and of acquaintanceship unto those who in confusion have transgressed. Support those who stumble, reach out your hand to the sick, feed those who are hungry, give repose to the weary, uplift those who yearn to arise, awaken those who sleep-for you are the wisdom that rescues!

35. Thus strength grows in action. Give heed to yourselves-be not concerned with those other things which you have already cast out of yourselves. Do not return to what you have regurgitated, be not moth-eaten, be not worm-eaten – for you have already cast that out. Do not become a place for the Devil, for you have already eliminated him. Do not reinforce those things that made you stumble and fall. Thus is uprightness!

36. For someone who violates the Torah harms himself more than the judgement harms him. For he does his deeds illicitly, whereas he who is righteous does his deeds for the sake of others. Do therefore the volition of the Father, because you are from Him. For the Father is kind, and things are good thru His volition. He has taken cognizance of whatever is yours, so that you may repose yourselves concerning such things-for in their fruition it is recognized whose they are.

37. The Sons of the Father are His fragrance, for they are from the grace of His face. Therefore the Father loves His fragrance and manifests it everywhere. And blending it with matter, He bestows His fragrance upon the light, and in His repose He exalts it over every likeness and every sound. For it is not the ears that inhale the fragrance, but rather the breath has the sense of smell and draws it to oneself – and thus is someone baptized in the fragrance of the Father.

38. Thus He brings it to harbor, drawing His original fragrance which had grown cold unto the place from which it came. It was something which in psychic form had become like cold water permeating loose soil, such that those who see it think it to be dirt. Then afterwards, when a warm and fragrant breeze blows, it again evaporates. Thus coldness results from separation. This is why the Faithful-One came-to abolish division and bring the warm fullness of love, so that the cold would not return but rather there should be the unification of perfect thought. This is the Logos of the Gospel of the finding of the fullness by those who await the salvation which comes from on High. Prolonged is the hope of those who await – those whose likeness is the light which contains no shadow – at that time when the fullness finally comes.

39. The deficiency of matter did not originate thru the infinity of the Father, who came in the time of inadequacy – although no one could predict that the indestructible would arrive in this manner. But the profundity of the Father abound, and the thought of confusion was not with him. It is a topic for falling prostrate, it is a reposeful topic – to be set upright on one's feet, in being found by this-One who came to bring him back. For the return is called: Metanoia!

40. This is why imperishability breathed forth – to seek after the transgressor so that he might have repose. For to forgive is to remain behind with the light, the Logos of the fullness, in the deficiency. Thus the physician hastens to the place where there is illness, for this is his heart's desire. But he who has a lack cannot hide it from him who possesses what he needs. Thus the fullness, which has no deficiency, replenishes the lack.

41. The Father gave of Himself to replenish whomever lacks, in order that thereby he may receive grace. In the time of his deficiency he had no grace. Thus wherever grace is absent, there is inferiority. At the time when he received this smallness which he lacked, then the Father revealed to him a fullness, which is the finding of the light of truth that dawned upon him in unchangeability. This is why the Christ was invoked in their midst-so that they would receive their returning. He anoints with the Chrism those who have been troubled. The anointing is the compassion of the Father who will have mercy upon them. Yet those whom He has anointed are those who are perfected.

42. For jars which are full are those which are sealed. Yet when its sealant is destroyed, a jar leaks. And the cause of its being emptied is the absence of its sealant, for then something in the dynamics of the air evaporates it. But that is not emptied

from which no sealant has been removed, nor does anything leak away, but rather the perfect Father replenishes whatever is lacking.

43. He is good. He knows His seedlings, for it is He who planted them in His paradise. Now His paradise is His realm of repose. This is the perfection in the thought of the Father, and these are the Logoi of His meditation. Each one of His Logoi is the product of His unitary volition in the revelation of His meaning. While they were still in the depths of His thought, the Logos was the first to come forth. Furthermore He revealed them from a mind that expresses the unique Logos in the silent grace called thought, since they existed therein prior to becoming manifest. So it occurred that the Logos was the first to come forth at the time when it pleased the volition of Him who intended it.

44. Now the volition of the Father is that which reposes in His heart and pleases Him. Nothing exists without Him, nor does anything occur without the volition of the Father. But His volition is unfathomable. His volition is His imprint, and no one can determine it nor anticipate it in order to control it. But whenever he wills, what He wills exists – even if the sight does not please them. They are nothing before the face of God and the volition of the Father. For he knows the beginning and the ending of them all – at their end He shall question them face-to-face. Yet the ending is to receive acquaintance with this-One who is hidden. Now this is the Father—this-One from whom the beginning came forth, this-One to whom all these shall return who came forth from Him. Yet they have been manifest for the glory and joy of His Name.

45. Now the Name of the Father is the Son. He first named Him who came forth from Himself, and who is Himself. And He begot Him as a Son. He bestowed His own Name upon Him. It is the Father who from His heart possesses all things. He has the Name, He has the Son who can be seen. Yet His Name is transcendental - for it alone is the mystery of the invisible, which thru Him comes to ears completely filled with it.

46. For indeed the Name of the Father is not spoken, yet rather it is manifested as a Son. Accordingly, great is the Name! Who therefore could proclaim a Name for Him, the Supreme Name, except Him alone whose Name this is, together with the Sons of the Name?- those in whose heart the Name of the Father reposes and who themselves likewise repose in His Name. Because the Father is unchangeable, it is He alone who begot Him as His own Name before He fashioned the Eternal-Ones, so that the Name of the Father would be Lord over their heads – this-One who is truly the Name, secure in His command of perfect power.

47. The Name is not mere wordage, nor is it only terminology, but rather it is transcendental. He alone named Him, He alone seeing Him, He alone having the power to give Him a name. Whoever does not exist has no name – for what names are given to nothingness? But this existing-One exists together with His Name. And the Father alone knows Him, and He alone names Him.

48. The Son is His Name. He did not keep Him hidden as a secret - but rather the Son came to be, and the Father alone named Him. Thus the Name belongs to the Father, such that the Name of the Father is the Son. How otherwise would compassion find a Name, except from the Father? For after all, anyone will say to his companion: 'Whoever could give a name to someone who existed before him? – as if children do not thus receive their names thru those who gave them birth!'

49. Firstly, therefore, it is appropriate that we think on this topic: what is the Name? Truly the Son is the Name – thus also He is the Name from the Father. He is the existent Name of the Lord. Thus He did not receive the Name on loan as do others, according to the pattern of each individual who is to be created in His heart. For He is the Lordly Name. There is no one else who bestowed it upon Him, but He unnamable and it was ineffable until the time when He who is Perfect gave expression to the Son alone. And it is the Son who has the power to express His Name and to see Him. Thus it pleased the Father in His heart that His desired Name be His Son, and He gave the Name to him – this-One who came forth from the profundity.

50. The Son expressed His secret, knowing that the Father is benevolent. This is exactly why the Father brought this-One forth-so that He might speak of the dominion and His place of repose from which He came, and render glory to the fullness, the majesty of His name, And the kindness of the Father. He shall speak of the realm from which each one came – and each one who issued from that place shall thus be hastened to return unto it again, to share in receiving His substance in the place where He stood, receiving the taste of that place, receiving nourishment and growth. And His own dominion of repose is His fullness.

51. Thus all the emanations of the Father are plenitudes, and the source of all His emanations is within the heart of Him from whom they all flourish. He bestowed their destinies upon them. Thus is each one made manifest, such that thru their own meditation they returned to the place to which they direct their thought. That place is their source, which lifts them thru all the heights of heaven unto the Father. They attain unto His head, which becomes their repose. And they are embraced as they approach Him, so that they say that they have partaken of His face in embraces. Yet they are not thus made manifest by exalting themselves. They neither lack the glory of the Father, nor do they think of Him as being trite or bitter or wrathful. But rather He is benevolent, imperturbable and kind – knowing all the dimensionalities before they come into existence, and having no need of edification.

52. This is the form of those who themselves belong on high thru the grandeur of the immeasurable, as they await the single and perfect-One who makes Himself there for them. And they do not descend unto the abode of the dead. They have neither jealousy nor lamentation nor mortality there among them, but rather

they repose within Him who is reposeful. They are neither troubled nor devious concerning the truth, but rather they themselves are the truth. The Father is within them and they are within the Father, perfected and made indivisible in the truly good, not inadequate in anything but rather given repose and refreshed in the Spirit. And they shall obey their source in leisure, these within whom His root is found and who harm no soul. This is the place of the blest, this is their place!

53. Wherefore let the remainder understand in their places that it is not appropriate for me, having been in the realm of repose, to say anything further. But it is within His heart that I shall be – forever devoted to the Father of the totality, together with those true Brothers upon whom pours the love of the Father and among whom there is no lack of Him. These are they who are genuinely manifest, being in the truth and eternal life and speaking the perfect light which is filled with the seed of the Father, and who are in His heart and in the fullness and in whom His Spirit rejoices, glorifying Him in whom they exist. He is good, and His Sons are perfect and worthy of His Name. For it is children of this kind that He the Father desires.

GLOSSARY

(For certain words used in all three Gospel accounts.)

Coptic was the final stage of the classical Egyptian language, evolving after the invasion of Alexander the Great (332 BC) and subsequently supplanted by Arabic following the Muslim conquest (640 AD). It has always been the liturgical language of the Egyptian Church; moreover, the ancient Coptic versions of the Old and New Testaments are of great importance in textual Biblical studies. It is also noted that during the times that Jesus was alive that the people of the region spoke Aramaic along with Latin and Greek.

Utilizing many Greek loan words, Coptic also adopted the Greek Alphabet (with C for Sigma and W for omega), adding these letters: 3 (shai), 4(fai), 2 (hori), 8 (janja), 6 (gima), 7 (ti), and – (syllable or abbreviation indicator).

Abraham: Hebrew (father of many); the first Hebrew patriarch [Gen. 11:26].

Adam: Hebrew (blood red, clay) –the original human and / or generic mankind.

Aeon: Coptic ENE2– Greek AIWN (unconditional); designates either a specific limited era of time, or a transtemporal eternity.

All: See Totality.

Angel: Greek AGGELOS – Hebrew MALAK (emissary, messenger); here the pure ego of the individual, born of God, who observes the images; Mt 18:10, Lk 20:36.

Anointed: Hebrew MASHIAKH (Messiah) – Greek CRISTOS; in ancient Israel priests and prophets and monarchs were installed by crowning with an olive-oil ointment (Ex 29:7, 1st Ki 19:16, 2nd Sam 2:4 – hence Lk 4:18, Mt 26:6-7); see Gen. 28:18, Ex 30:20-33.

Apostle: Greek APOSTOLOS (sent forth); one who is commissioned; compare Disciple.

Apostolic: Greek APOSTOLIKOS (follower of the Apostles).

Aramaic: Semitic language of the ancient world, dated by extra-Biblical records to 3000 BC, source of Hebrew square-letter alphabet, the language of Abraham (Dt 26:5) as well as of Christ in His ministry (Mk 5:41, 7:34, 15:34, Mt 27:46); Gen. 22:20-21, 2nd Ki 18:26, Isa 36:11.

Atone: Coptic SWTE – Greek LUTROW –Hebrew KPR 9Cover, substitute; as in 'Yom Kippur': Day of Atonement); personal sacrifice or suffering, by the guilty or the innocent, which serves to reconcile the quilty (Lev 1:1-4, 16:1-34, Isa 53, Mt 5:10-12, 20:28); see Sacrament.

Authority: Greek ARCWN (original-being); an official within the system.

Baptism: Greek BAPTISMA (immersion); the sacrament of spiritual cleansing re the Torah --see Sacrament, Torah, Isa 1:16-17, Mk1:4, Mt 28:19, Ac 1:22.

Bear: Interpolated Coptic text, TA, MAAU, GAR, NTA MISE, MMO, OL "my mother did-[she –bear, accusative-me forth]; papyrus.

Bed: The Coptic text here is: A.K.TELO (did-thou [masc] –lay)(upon)(my-bed)- this last is the one and only Sahidic Coptic word for 'bed'; it does not mean 'sofa', (place of reclining), Gen. 48:2, Ex 21:18, Job 7:13, Ps 36:4, 63:6, Prov 7:16-17, Mk 2:4, 4:21, Lk 7:14, Jn 5:8, Ac 5:15 –thus in the Sahidic version of Ac 5:15.

Bedroom: Greek KOITWN.

Blest: Greek MAKARIOS; which means divine, rather than merely human, beatitude (Mt 5:3 ET passim).

Breath: See Spirit.

Bridal-Chamber: Coptic MA n. 3ELEET (place of-bride); Greek NUMFWN – Hebrew KHEDER; the bedroom where the marriage is consummated (Jud 15:1, Ps 19:5, 45: 13-15, S-of-S 1:4, Jn 3:29, Mt 9:15 [OI YIOI TOY NUMFWNOS, the Sons of the Bridal-Chamber] 25:1-13)

Cain: Hebrew (product and hence possession), that is, 'my or our work' rather than 'work of God', perhaps indicating that the 'original transgression' of humans consisted in claiming (Godlike) to create, and hence to judge, their offspring; Gen. 2:15-4:1, Ecl 11:5 – see 'Theogenesis'.

Chrism: Greek CRISMA (unguent) – Coptic NE, SON, TWS; the sacrament of anointing with olive oil, christification; see Anointed, Sacrament.

Christ: Greek CRISTOS; see Anointed.

Christic: Greek CRISTIKOS (follower of Christ) - Hebrew 'Messianic'(follower of the Messiah).

Clergy: Aramaic PERUSHIM ('Pharisees': separated); religious leaders; Mt 5:20, 23:1-39, etc.

Communion: Coptic 3LHL; communicating with God, prayer (note that in Lk 18:1, PANTOTE PROSEUCESQAI means pray continually).

Confusion: Greek PLANH (straying; hence 'planet' as a celestial body which appears to stray relative to the fixed stars).

Contemplation: Greek QEWRIA; here meaning to behold one's imagery as God's own manifested imagination (Mt 18:10).

Convocation: Greek EKKLHSIA (called out); the assembly of those 'called forth' from the world (Mt 16:18, 18:15-20); this had been the term for the Athenian Assembly; Ps 22:22.

<u>Count:</u> This refers to the ancient technique of finger-calculation, whereby numbers 1-99 were counted on the left hand but from 100 upward on the right hand; the number 100 itself was formed by touching the right forefinger-tip to the upper joint of the thumb.

<u>Dead, Abode of:</u> Coptic EMNTE (west, as the entrance to the underworld) – Hebrew SHEOL (plead) – Greek AIDHS (Hades: 'unseen').

<u>Defilement:</u> Coptic 8W2M = Greek MIASMA = Hebrew TAME; ritual uncleanness (as in Leviticus 15), as opposed to transgression of the Torah (as in Leviticus 19) – a vital distinction; see Torah, compare with transgression.

<u>Disciple:</u> Greek MAQHTHS (learner); in Attic Greek, used of the pupils of the philosophers and rhetoricians, compare Apostle.

<u>Disparity:</u> Coptic AT.TWT; not in agreement, not conjoined.

<u>Emanation:</u> Convincingly shows that this term is analogous to the Neo-Platonic notion of divine radiation, wherein all beings are likened to sunbeams emanating from the one God; see Plotinus, Enneads: 'The analogy of the light from a sun – the entire intellectual order may be figured as a kind of light, with the One in repose at its summit as its King'. Christ says that He is the son of God, and this means that He emanates from God.

<u>Entice:</u> Coptic SOK (to blow as the wind or to flow as water, hence to draw or attract.) Greek ELKW.

<u>Eternal:</u> See Aeon.

<u>Eternal-Ones:</u> All creatures considered as eternal, relative to the trans-dimensional mind of God.

<u>Eucharist:</u> Greek EUCARISTIA (well-joying, thanksgiving); the sacrament of bread and wine.

<u>Eve:</u> Hebrew (living); see Cain and Female.

<u>Everything:</u> See Totality.

<u>Expectation:</u> Greek ELPIS = Hebrew TIQVAH; not mere hoping or wishing, but rather anticipation – thus Clement of Alexandria, Stromata: 'Hope is the expectation of the possession of good; necessarily, then, is expectation founded on faith'.

<u>Female:</u> Coptic S2IME; here emphasizing the Holy Spirit as our Mother; see Spirit.

<u>Form:</u> Latin FORMA; it is a noteworthy idiosyncrasy of this text that the Latin term is employed rather than the Greek MORFH.

<u>Gnostic:</u> Hidden knowledge, secret knowledge. See also Incarnate and Recognition. 'Gnosticism' is by definition metaphysically Platonic, maintaining that both the sensory universe and all incarnation are illusory; these gospels, contrarily, share the Biblical view that both the perceptual universe and all incarnations are divinely created.

<u>Heaven:</u> See Sky.

<u>Hebrew:</u> Hebrew EBER (cross over, beyond, passer-by, transient): the lineage of Shem and especially of Abraham, thus Ishmael also was a Hebrew.

<u>Heir:</u> Progeny.

<u>Holy Spirit:</u> Hebrew RUAKH HA-QODESH (Spirit the –Holy; feminine gender) = Greek PNEUMA TO AGION 9 neuter gender) = Coptic P.PNEUMA ET.QUAAB (masculine gender; as also Latin SPIRITUS SANCTUS)

<u>Image / Imagery:</u> Greek EIKON (similitude) = Hebrew TSELEM (shadow); sensory perceptions and / or mental images, the five senses together with memory and the imagination.

<u>Incarnate:</u> Coptic 2N SARX (in flesh).

Ionian: Greek IONIOS (violet) = Hebrew JAVAN / YAYIN (wine); Hebrew name for the Greeks, the coast of Asia Minor (now Turkey) was where Greeks met the ancient middle-eastern civilizations, acquiring the alphabet via the Semitic-speaking Phoenicians FOINIX (purple – Greek name for the Canaanites, Hebrew: 'merchants'.

Jacob the Righteous: Hebrew YAKOV (heeler, supplanter) = Greek IAKWBOS = English 'James', Christ's human brother.

Jerusalem: Hebrew (foundation / city of peace); Hebrew YARAH (directive) is the root of both 'Jeru' and 'Torah'.

John the Baptist: John = Hebrew (Yah is merciful), the last Hebrew prophet and the Messianic precursor to and 2nd cousin of Jesus. See oracle.

Jordan: Hebrew (descender); the river of the Holy Land, in the northern extension of Africa's Great Rift Valley; apparently the River Pishon of Gen. 2:11).

Joseph the Craftsman: Joseph = Hebrew (addition); craftsman = Coptic 2AM3E, Greek TEKTWN. Surname Jaccoba.

King: See Vintage.

Levi: Hebrew (join, convert); the Old Testament patriarch of the priestly line.

Logi: Greek LOGOI; this is the plural of Logos (see Saying/Meaning), indicating that each Son - or – Daughter of God is a divine Logos like unto the Savior.

Lord/Master: Hebrew ADON = Greek KURIOS = Coptic 8OEIS; owner of a slave.

Magdalene: Hebrew MIGDAL (great, watchtower); being of the town of Magdalah.

Manifest: Coptic OUWN2 EBOL (show forth – in the transitive and non-reflective sense, indicating which is both beyond itself and unperceived.

Mariam: Hebrew MROM (exalted); five females named Miriam appeared in the Gospels: the Virgin, Miriam of Magdalah, Miriam of Bethany, Miriam of Cleopas, and the Lord's human sister – Miriam Jaccoba.

Mate: Greek KOINWNIA (common-being); sexual union. Israelite 'concubinage', a non-marital sexual union (in which the offspring do not inherit), as Abraham with Hagar and Ketura, forbidden neither by the Torah nor by Christ, (although adultery refer only to the wife of another man, not to an unmarried woman or a widow).

Matthew: Hebrew MATTAN-YAH (gift of Yah); the Apostle and Evangelist, also named 'Levi of Alphaeus', brother of the Apostle Jacob of Alphaeus.

Meaning: See Saying.

Measurement: Hebrew M-SHQL (of-weighing, shekel) is apparently here being punned with MASHIAKH (Messiah).

Messiah: Hebrew MASHIAKH; see Anointed.

Messianic: Hebrew 'Messiah' with Greek suffix –IKOS; thus 'follower of the Messiah' – see Christic.

Metanoia: See Rethink.

Midst: Coptic MHTE (amidst, in transition hence this transitory world); see Transition.

Mode: Greek EIDOS (form); the term for the Platonic forms (often as IDEA) as well as the Aristotelian species; note also the evident allusion to the four primary elements of ancient physics: earth, water, air and fire (recast in modern formulation as the four basic states of matter: solid, liquid, gas and Plasma).

Mystery: Greek MUSTHRION (secret or sacrament, a term from the ancient Mediterranean 'Mystery Religions'); see Sacrament.

Nationalist: Greek EQNIKOS = Hebrew GOY (corpse!); non-Israelite, pagan, Gentile.

Natural: See Vintage/Kind.

Nazarene: Hebrew 'of Nazareth' (New Testament Greek spelling NAZARHNOS); to be carefully distinguished from:

Nazarite: Hebrew (crowned, consecrated); Greek spelling NAZWRAIOS, Hebrew holy man or woman with uncut hair, abstaining from products of the grapevine, and avoiding corpses – the latter two rules of which Christ implicitly abrogated.

Novice: Greek PROSHLUTOS (Proselyte, toward-comer); a Torah convert, such as St. Nicolas of Antioch ('Santa Claus', the first Gentile Disciple!).

Ointment: The Chrism or oil of anointing; see Chrism.

Oracle/Prophet: Greek PROFHTHS = Hebrew NABI; a divine spokesperson, not merely predictive; note that there are 24 books in the Hebrew canon of the old testament, and also 24 Prophets including John the Baptist.

Origin: Greek ARCH; a term from the pre-Socratic Greek philosophers, meaning not a temporal beginning but rather the primal source or basic substance underlying reality.

Paradise: Greek PARADEISOS; Persian word meaning 'garden/park'; Old Testament depiction of the garden that was husbanded by Adam and Eve. 'So He drove out the man; and He placed at the east of the garden of Eden Cherubims, and a flaming sword which turned every way, to keep the way of the tree of life. (Note) Mount Mariah is where the tree of life was in the midst of Eden.

Passer-by: Greek PARAGEIN (by-led); transient, itinerant – see Hebrew.

Paul: Latin 'small'; the supposed Apostle, remarkably, Matthew 5:19 can thus be read 'Whoever relaxes one of the least of these commandments [much less all of them, as per Romans 7:6!]...shall be called Paul (i.e. small) in the Kingdom of Heaven.'

Perfect: Greek TELEIOS (completed); biblical morality exhibits a three-valued rather than a binary logic: (1) evil/wrong [in violation of the Torah], (2) good/right [in accordance with the Torah], and (3) perfect [in accordance with the Messiah]; see Matthew 5:48 19:16-21.

Philip The Apostle: Philip = Greek FILOS-IPPOS ->FILIPPOS: friend of horses, to be distinguished from:

Philip The Evangelist: (Colophon): author of this text.

Philosopher: Greek FIROSOFOS (fond of wisdom); this word (coined by the pre-Socratic Pythagoras) has no precise Hebrew/Aramaic equivalent, and thus Matthew himself may have used the Greek term; but see the parallel at Job 9:4, Hebrew KHAKAM LIBA (wise in heart).

Prophet: See Oracle.

Prostitution: Greek PORNEIA (from PERNHMI, to sell) does not mean 'fornication' (non-adulterous sexual relations outside of marriage, including importantly a concubine [Hebrew PILEGESH] as in Genesis 16:3 & 25:6) but rather 'prostitution' (cultic or commercial sexual relations, as in pornography'); prostitution is forbidden by Deuteronomy 23:17 (cultic) & Leviticus 19:29 (commercial) – note that the blame falls solely on her parents, her procurer and her clients, and not on the prostitute herself, who is a victim, interestingly, in biblical times only harlots wore veils.

Rabbi: Hebrew (my great-one) = Coptic NO6 (great, C25O); a spiritual authority.

Rebirth: Coptic 8PO.N.KE.SOP (birth another time;) not = Greek GENETH ANWQEN (generation from above [up-place]; the Greek can equally mean 'birth from above' or 'birth again'.

Recognize: See Rethink.

Recognition: Coptic SOOUN; Greek GNWSIS (gnosis); this important term means direct personal acquaintance rather than mere intellectual knowledge. Incarnate and Gnosticism.

Rethink: Greek METANOEW (be with-mind, be wholeminded, after-mind, reconsider) = Hebrew SHUB (return), the initial message of both John the Baptist and Christ; this important term 'metanoia' (mindfulness) contrasts with 'paranoia' (beside-mind, mindlessness) – it does not signify a mere feeling of remorse, which is METAMELOS (with/after-sentiment).

Sabbath: Hebrew SHABAT (repose); the (7th) day of rest; Saturday.

Sacrament: See Mystery; Philip 73 gives a hierarchical list of five Sacraments: (1) Baptism [personal moral cleansing re the Torah]; (2) Chrism [the Messianic Discipleship]; (3) Eucharist [the communal meal, commemorating Yeshua's sacrifice]; (4) Atonement [suffering for the salvation of others: persecution, empathy]; and (5) Holy Bridal-Chamber [the uniting of the male with the female Disciples, to celebrate their eternal birth thru the mating of the Father with the Spirit].

Salome: Hebrew SHLOMIT (peaceful); Yeshua's oldest stepsister, also a Disciple.

Samaritan: Those Hebrews not deported to Babylon and hence lacking the later Old Testament scriptures, therefore in post-Exilic times considered heretics due to intermingled blood with other non-Hebrew people. Considered dogs by the Hebrew.

Savior: Greek SWTHR = Coptic NOU2M = Hebrew YASHA; see Yeshua.

Saying/Meaning: Coptic 3A8E = Greek LOGOS = Hebrew AMR = Aramaic MEMRA; English 'meaning' derives from Anglo-Saxon 'maenan' = 'to have in mind, mention, conceive + express', the exact sense of both Logos and Memra; John 1:1 thus reads 'In (the) Origin was the Meaning'; one Greek term for 'word' is RHMA.

Scheme: Greek SXHMA (form, plan, and appearance as opposed to the substantial reality).

Seal: Coptic TBBE; s sealant such as retsina, used to affix the top onto a jar/amphora to make it airtight (perhaps led to the tradition of retsina flavoring in Greek wine).

Shimon Kefa: Hebrew SHIMON = hearing; Aramaic KEFA = Greek PETROS (bedrock) – after Christ's death and resurrection, became the chief Apostle, Simon Peter.

Sky/Heaven: Coptic PE = Greek OURANOS = Hebrew SHAMAYIM (plural); note that 'heaven' = 'sky' in all three languages.

Spirit: Hebrew RUAKH (feminine gender!) = Greek PNEUMA (neuter gender!); in both languages the word for 'spirit' is like 'breath' or 'wind', see Holy Spirit.

Symbol: Greek TUPOS (type, alphabetical letter, pattern, model, general idea).

System: See World.

Theologian: Greek GRAMMATEUS (scribe); an expert on the scriptures.

Thomas: Aramaic TAOM (twin) = Greek DIDUMOS; the youngest brother of Yeshua, also named Judas in the Hebrew (praised), the Apostle Thomas, the author of this text.

Torah: Hebrew (arrow, directive); the 613 commandments or mitzvot of the Old Testament Law, also specifically the five books of Moses.

Totality: Coptic THR-4 (all/every of-Him); everyone, everything, the All.

Transgression: Coptic NOBE = Greek AMARTIA = Hebrew KHATAT; a violation of the Torah, a sin, see Torah and Defilement.

Transition: Coptic MHTE = Greek MESOTHS (middle); between alternatives, neither the one nor the other.

Trees: The 'five trees' may refer to the five senses (that all emotions can presumably be included in the realm of feeling), it is noteworthy that the olive tree in particular does not shed its leaves annually.

Trust: Greek PISTIS (trust, faith); not mere factual opinion, but rather personal confidence in someone or something.

Unite: Coptic TW2 (combine or couple, copulate); first, Matthew 19:12 in the context of the previous four Sacraments, and only then the fifth Sacrament!; see Mate and Sacrament.

Vintage/Kind/Natural: Greek (used), the ancient pagans often confused this common term with the rare CRISTOS, with reference to the Hebrew Messiah.

War: Greek POLEMOS; perhaps it is logical nowadays to interpret 'the stars falling from the sky' (Mark 13:25, Revelations 6:13 & 8:5-11) as a nuclear war, since hydrogen bombs are literally small man-made stars; 'this generation' in Mark 13:30 is presumably counted from either May 1948 (the refounding of Israel) or June 1967 (the reconquest of Jerusalem, Luke 21:24), and could range from forty years (Numbers 14:33, Deuteronomy 2:14) to one hundred years (Genesis 15:13-16).

Wickedness: Greek PONEROS; this term (which also occurs in the canonical Gospels at Mark 7:22-23 etc.) has a root meaning of hard work or laborious drudgery, thus oppressive or exploitative.

World/System: Greek KOSMOS (arrangement, order) – originally the pre-Socratic philosopher Pythagoras had used this term to designate the entire natural universe, as in 'comos'; but in the gospel koine (later common Greek) it had also come to signify the conventionality or artificiality of the human social system, as in 'cosmetic'.

Yeshua: Hebrew YHOSHUA (YOD. HE.VAV.SHIN.VAV.AYIN); from YHWH YSHA (He-Is Savior); Aramaic YSHUA (YOD.SHIN.VAV.AYIN).

Notes

Chapter 9

THESE ARE A FEW of the sayings that I have developed over the years. Some may seem like rambling, but under the right circumstances they will make perfect sense. It is my hope that some of these may help you in your walk through life.

This is basically just a break from the heavy informational reading load that you have been exposed to. These are...

DraVerbs

1. It is better to know than not to know.
2. If we could just get over our laziness, we could do anything. Work It Now! Stop fearing to do Effort. Fear is of the enemy, FIGHT the enemy or die.
3. Instead of paying attention to the 'little what's so wrong' (nit picking), you should be paying attention to the 'big what's going on'.
4. Don't think little, think large. But make it simple although it looks complex.
5. Most supervisors are the types of people who would remove the chocolate chips out of the cookie, leaving nothing but crumbs, while missing the point of value.
6. Information: I'm smart enough to obtain it, and dangerous enough to use it.
7. Take hold of anything that is good that you find in any place that may help you help others, because, life works better when you can make someone's life a little bit better, whether with a smile or a comforting or an inspiring word.
8. An affirmation to consider: I must begin to be successful, by doing successful things. Avoiding mistakes and overcoming obstacles. If things are going wrong, examine the problem, examine the causes, mentally examine the possible cures and plans of action. Work the plan of action; if one plan don't cure the problem, use another. All problems are plainly showing the answer, choose the right answer, and the problem will turn into success instead of simply being a problem. But don't be fooled into believing that a problem will go away if it's ignored or can be wished away. A problem covered only festers and grows worst. OBSERVATION, EXAMINATION, CAREFUL PLANNING, PROPER DISICIONS, and ACTION are the ways to dominate any problem.

9. Don't panic and get so frustrated when problems arise, those things don't make the problems more easier, but only makes them harder to solve, because they take you out of the proper frame of mind to be a Problem Solver.

10. The most valuable asset to any company is for you to be a Problem Solver as well as an inspired employee who always look for the good and positive in all matters.

11. Don't forget to be persistent and determined.

12. Break it down-like-art-work...that's what I better do...in other words, dissect it like a scientist.

13. No matter how quick or slow...flowing movement-nonstop, even at touch points, as to roll of f of it, like it's just another point of the timeframe, not really paid attention to, because it's on a higher level of thought, I see it but it is only to pick it out of the chain of events to stop and look at it in what seems a long time but it's only a piece of a second and your mind clicked through its time, the time before and the time after, and all you did was stop and recognize the thought...and with others hearing at their bewilderment, and...the flow is interrupted only to either try and start over...or just move on flowing in some new direction...although, no direction is new, it just starts over.

14. If you are thinking about doing a thing, you ought to make up your mind if you are going to do it, or not do it. Then begin to pursue it with the burning desire to accomplish it as if you are in pursuit of the intense feeling of release as in the sexual experience or not pursue it and avoid the thought as though it was a contagious disease.

15. You better wake up, so that you'll know where you belong. There are <u>ONLY</u> two sides, which side are you on.

16. It's not what you do, but What you do, that determines who you are in our vision.

17. God never said that on this earth in your life it will ever get to the point where you can expect your life to be working as well as you would expect it to and not be full of drama that was not expected, because no matter how long you live, the next thing to happen in your life just hadn't been written yet but it's expected that each second you live you really will not know what to expect next...because it hasn't happened before don't mean that it's not coming...expect and prepare mentally and physically for the unexpected...and even if it happened before, it can happen again.

18. "Why" is the question that brings the most answers and is the quickest way to halt answers from those of weak intelligence. In learning something, always search for the 'WHY'.

19. Once you figure it out, it comes as no surprise when disguised in another form. It's still the same ol' thing.

20. Fear is based on lack of knowledge, but knowledge acquired eliminates fear although caution may remain.

21. As of now, the only thing that can't be done is to walk on water, some day it will be possible, but right now, all things are possible to those who conceives a plausible idea, believe it can be accomplished and works to achieve that possibility.

22. Put your brain to work.

23. Are your words harmful to others and yourself? Change your way of thinking by first examining the things you say, three days later, begin your transformation. But you must want to change your persona for the better in order to be able to maintain your progress.

24. If you find yourself criticizing others, it's only because you see yourself in their actions wile they go through the particular situations that causes you to criticize them. You are really only criticizing yourself.

25. Really successful men all over the world are too honorable to waste time gloating over their personal triumphs.

26. Most people are afraid of information if it's not entertainment and if it's correction for their faults, then their goal is containment.

27. Who's in control of you, your mind or your flesh? (Either ME, MYSELF or I, is in charge of all, so who is behind the steering wheel of you). Control your desire to lie. Remember; for some reason, being nice to unbelievers tend to make them target you for an attack later. The answer to why is within the problem. After the attack whether successful or not, they tend to seek approval through lather and mundane conversation with others, but they still watch for your reaction. It makes them glad to see you distressed, mad or upset and it causes them fear almost to the point of panic to see you still smiling, unfazed and still upbeat in your attitude. Their uneasiness will almost be to the point that they'll find any reason to be out of your presence if only for a little while. You may have to approach them first for any type of transaction afterwards.

28. As it takes great strength to be totally ruthless, it takes even greater strength to be perfect, and maintain it minute after minute, everyday. When you're close, the weak people who are no where near your level, try to enhance whatever flaw they see or can find about you. The darkness cannot see in the light, so it seeks out darkness about the past of one who left darkness to become light. It attacks the new in the old ways in desperate attempts to bring the light back into being darkness.

29. Have you ever made a mistake whether on purpose or accidentally? Then why be so hard on the young ones for their faults, explain it to them, discipline them strongly, (until age 14-physically whip their butt, and not in a weak manner) and then trust their judgment to make better decisions as they grow. But realize that there will be times when disappointment will occur.

30. A child, (male and female), should begin to learn to bake, cook, do laundry, learn business principles, be taught to pay for services and receive the change back after paying, and be taught etiquette principles beginning at five years of age. These skills should be mastered by the age of fourteen. This is how to produce outstanding members of society. Its called HOME TRAINING. Try it. Be the PARENT, it's your roll.

31. Darkness will little by little become more darkness without any effort, light coming out of darkness does so little by little by effort until the distressing of the darkness becomes more and more to the changing of the darkness around it, either to grow as light or to grow more into darkness.

32. If it is what I am to be, I will not be a weak one.

33. Waiting on others can be a long wait, doomed to their timing. Use what you have to get what you need in order to not have to depend on the lackadaisicalness of others.

34. When you are not speaking, focus your mind into prayer, you will see how it keeps you moving into the Light.

35. There are some around you who desire to have control over you, they will use fear tactics to stymie you in your progress, creativity, adventures, and ideas, such as to say, 'You can't...' or 'They wont let you...' or 'They will kill/hurt you for that idea...' and many other "Fear For You" type statements. Smile at their attempts to "try to help you" and use your positive affirmations and actions to move ahead, but still use caution and not go into the matter blindly.

36. What do you enjoy doing? Maybe that is something that you can do in a business for yourself.

37. Camouflage works great! Being light since defecting from the darkness, knowledge of the darkness can be used against it. Of another Kingdom among those of this system on earth.

38. It is a dangerous thing to offend the Children of the Light, although the children of the darkness don't realize it because lots of times there are no immediate repercussions that they can relate to.

39. Sometimes people just need an ear to bend, and if you really pay attention, it will be rather easy to give good solid advice. You will be appreciated and called on again later by them or someone that they recommend.

40. Listen twice as much as you speak. There are some people who barley take a breath while speaking extremely long sentences that change from subject to subject to subject while not giving you a chance to respond to anything that they have said already...(in/exhaling...wwehooooooo!).

41. Stay young, time is the only movement superficially, temporary yet undenighably degeneratively to the flesh, mind and spirit. Strengthen the brain continuously through learning and righteous living to renew your being.

42. Can you be someone who see things as God made and not as good or evil, except to see true evil as true evil and good that would be considered evil as only corrupted by evil?

43. Darkness makes that way of life looks extremely enticing but what's not realized is destruction is the end result, only the realization is not realized until its too late. As it is written, 'The wages of sin is death.' Don't you want to receive your pay for the work that you have done?

44. There are times when you will hear someone say, 'This place is better than that place, or here is better, harder, more dangerous, more competitive and etc. than there…' However, I say, 'If you can walk here, you can walk anywhere. You will find DalWorth everywhere you go!'

45. When we are young we feel almost indestructible and can't see ourselves in the failing portion of the older ones, but as my Mother use to say, 'Just keep on living and you will think differently later.'

The End

(Of the First Book)

Notes